DEATH on IONA

The Mysterious Death of Norah Fornario and the Search for Netta

Ben Oakley

SELECT TITLES BY BEN OAKLEY

FICTION

HARRISON LAKE INVESTIGATIONS
The Camden Killer
The Limehouse Hotel
Monster of the Algarve

SUBNET SF TRILOGY
Unknown Origin
Alien Network
Final Contact

NONFICTION

TRUE CRIME
Bizarre True Crime Series
Monsters of True Crime
Orrible British True Crime Series
The Monstrous Book of Serial Killers
True Crime 365 series
Year of the Serial Killer

OTHER NONFICTION
Death on Iona
Suicide Prevention Handbook

The true evolutionary purpose of imagination is to enable the personality to quarry from the dull uninspiring grind of everyday life.

Norah Fornario, 1928.

Copyright © 2022 Ben Oakley.

First published in 2022 as 'The Immortal Hour' by Twelvetrees Camden.

This edition 2023.

The right of Ben Oakley to be identified as the
Author of the Work has been asserted by him in accordance
with the Copyright, Designs and Patents Act 1988.

Visit the author's website at www.writetheplanet.co.uk

All rights reserved. No part of this book may be reproduced, or stored in a
retrieval system, or transmitted in any form or by any means, electronic,
mechanical, photocopying, recording, or otherwise, without express written
permission of the publisher.

The book has been fully researched and fact-checked and all information is
correct at the time of publication. This book is meant for entertainment and
informational purposes only.

While the publisher and author have used their best efforts in preparing this
book, they make no representations or warranties with respect to the accuracy or
completeness of the contents of this book. Neither the publisher nor the author
shall be liable for any loss of profit or any other commercial damages, including
but not limited to special, incidental, consequential, personal, or other damages.

The author or publisher cannot be held responsible for any errors or
misinterpretation of the facts detailed within. The book is not intended to hurt or
defame individuals or companies involved.

ISBN: 978-1-915929-24-2

Cover artwork by Marina Luisa.

For information about special discounts available
for bulk purchases, sales promotions, book signings,
trade shows, and distribution, contact
hello@twelvetreescamden.co.uk

Twelvetrees Camden Ltd
71-75 Shelton Street, Covent Garden
London, WC2H 9JQ

www.twelvetreescamden.co.uk

Chapters

Acknowledgements...7

Introduction..9

The Search For God...11

The Curse of Osiris 17

The Voices of the Elemental Kingdoms 41

The Age of Influence..55

The Call of the Sacred Island..................................65

The Loneliness of Time...79

The Realm of the Dead...87

The Persistence of Myth 95

The Timeless Tale 113

The Lingering Mysteries 125

The Corridors of Time..135

The Legacy of Norah...139

The Immortal Hour 147

The Use of Imagination 163

Selected Bibliography 171

Acknowledgements

This book owes its existence to the kindness, patience, and generosity of many, including Mairi MacArthur, Michelle & Brent Salt, Georgia Satchel, Susan Windram, Jan Pickard, Daniela, Donna Wotherspoon, the team at Mull Museum, Police Scotland, Iona Abbey, Samuel Hatcher, Michael John Hymans, Alan Smith, Michael Ockenden, Wolf, Drew from The Keep archives, the freemasons archive and library, and Marina, my soulmate, as well as others who have preferred to remain anonymous but played a pivotal role in the book's research.

Death on Iona

Introduction

The enigmatic demise of Norah Fornario had long captured my imagination, particularly as I grew up fascinated by mysteries steeped in the occult and had spent time on Iona myself. This tragic tale has been discussed by spiritual scholars, mystery enthusiasts, and even in true crime circles.

Numerous blog posts, articles, and columns have recounted the story, but upon delving deeper, I found that many details had been misrepresented. One such inaccuracy involves the photograph of Norah frequently featured in blog posts, which is actually Moina Mathers, wife of Samuel Liddell MacGregor Mathers – a founder of the Hermetic Order of the Golden Dawn.

Another falsehood concerns the identity of Norah's host on Iona. Many sources name Mrs. MacRae, but it was, in fact, a family by the name of Cameron that welcomed her into their home. Norah stayed in their attic, and their children later shared recollections of her time there.

The purpose of this book is to present thoroughly researched material, facts, and information about the individuals on the periphery of Norah's life, enabling readers to draw their own conclusions after examining the evidence – and the absence thereof.

With a deep understanding of the occult, personal experiences of mental health struggles, and expertise in the psychology of crime and mystery, I strive to provide a logical explanation for the story of Norah Fornario.

This is the second, refined edition of the book, previously released as 'The Immortal Hour' in 2022. The initial release aimed to gauge interest and uncover any additional information regarding a life seemingly lost to history – and it succeeded in doing so.

Ultimately, this work is dedicated to honouring the memory of a young woman who lost herself between the thin veil separating worlds and the vast expanse of her own haunted heart.

Ben Oakley, Camden, London, May 2023

The Search For God

The tale that follows has its beginning, appropriately enough, in Hastings, the town where the occultist and magician Aleister Crowley had passed in 1947. It was there that I met Norah – not in person, but in the way so many thousands of people would meet her over the years; her death.

Nourished on a spiritualist blend of early 20th-century occultism and religious beliefs, I eagerly delved into the enigmatic world of the unknown and the ultimate quest we all embark upon in life – the search for God.

It was in Hastings, whilst researching the fantasy author David Gemmell, of all people, that I encountered the works of Dion Fortune and Madame Blavatsky, two influential writers whose legacies span a century of human history. Through Dion's writings, I was introduced to a certain Miss Fornario, now known to me as Norah.

In the early 20th century, Norah, one of our great lost intellects, sought solace from her loneliness and depression in places few dared to venture. Drawn to untold truths, she immersed herself in the heart of early

20th-century occultism, sheltered by the Golden Dawn and a level of spiritualism never before witnessed.

In the early autumn of 1929, the 33-year-old half-Italian, half-English writer left her opulent London home and set off for the remote Scottish island of Iona, the cradle of Christianity. She resided in the attic room of the Cameron house and spent her nights typing away. But Norah was no ordinary writer – she was an ex-member of the Alpha et Omega (Golden Dawn) occult order, an outer guardian of a co-masonic lodge, and an initiate of The Society of Inner Light.

Norah's life had been marked by grief, losing her mother and grandparents by the age of 12. Luckily, coming from a wealthy family, she attended private schools and inherited a substantial fortune from her grandfather. Over time, Norah came to view Iona as a "thin place," a location where the veil between the elemental world and the real one was tantalisingly close. She journeyed to Iona to write and experience the island's magic first-hand.

One fateful night, her hosts sought her out, but she was nowhere to be found. After a brief search along the moonlit shores, they retired for the night. The hunt for Norah resumed the following day, and almost two days later, two crofters discovered Norah's nude body on the rocks west of the island.

What transpired next is a mystery that has persisted for nearly a century. Norah's death has been sensationalised to such an extent that new blog posts emerge every month, perpetuating falsehoods surrounding the case and exacerbating the century-old cycle of rumours. This book examines all available research and proposed theories in an unbiased manner while debunking some of the inaccuracies found online.

Upon discovering some of Norah's writings under various pseudonyms, I was astounded by her extraordinary imagination and her command of the English language. My delight was tinged with sorrow when I learned that much of her work had been lost to history as Norah had succumbed to the eternal search for God.

Upon first learning of the enigmatic death of Norah Fornario, I, like many others, was captivated by the secretive elements surrounding the tale. A secluded Scottish island, a cryptic demise, ties to the occult, affiliations with mystical groups, and at the core of it all, a woman whose life – and death – were ultimately eclipsed by the embellishments that grew louder than her own remarkable voice.

Upon first hearing of Norah Fornario's mysterious death, I, like many others, was drawn to the intriguing elements surrounding the tale. From a secluded Scottish island to cryptic demise, ties to the occult, affiliations with mystical groups, and a woman whose life – and death – were ultimately overshadowed by embellishments that grew louder than her own remarkable voice.

Despite frequent blog posts and articles emerging every few months about her passing, they often focus on conjecture and baseless rumour rather than her life or the logic behind her fate. To truly comprehend our past and face the future, we must continuously explore and remember the memory of the deceased.

An image frequently attributed to Norah is, in fact, not her. Contrary to popular belief, she stayed with the Cameron family on Iona, not the MacRaes. More significantly, Norah rarely referred to herself as Netta – the name she is now widely known by. It was merely one of many exoticisms added throughout subsequent retellings.

It is worth noting that an image often attributed to Norah is not hers, and she stayed with the Cameron family on Iona, not the MacRaes. Additionally, Norah rarely referred to herself as Netta, contrary to popular belief.

The 1929 reports identified her as Norah or Nora, or simply Miss Fornario, and her surname was often misspelled. In a 1955 account, she was called Nessa. The name Netta first appeared in Francis King's 1970 book and has since been consistently used in various writings, although some argue that it served as a more exotic name for retelling the fantastic story that required a fitting moniker.

The truth is that Netta was a nickname she used in connection with a co-masonic group in London. Consulting with the archivist at the Freemason museum and library in London revealed that Netta Fornario was listed as Outer Guardian in the membership rolls of the Hammersmith co-masonic lodge during 1920/1921.

Although early literature mentions her Christian names, over the past century, the woman who perished on Iona has come to be known as Netta. While much has been written and speculated about her enigmatic death, this book delves deeply into the narrative, circumstances, and life of Norah Fornario, the real person behind the mystery.

Historical deaths often become fodder for present-day mystery and true crime aficionados, but the peculiar nature of Norah's demise primarily stems from later exaggerated accounts and Chinese whispers, which perpetuate erroneous truths and conspiracy theories.

Although Norah was an occult student and participated in the magical renaissance of the early 20th century, the enigma lies in why 21st-century bloggers have added fictitious elements to her story. These outlandish theories range from a Wicker Man-style island to claims that Aleister Crowley himself journeyed to Iona to "handle matters."

Yet, when confronted with something unexplained, we often resort to using our imagination to fill the gaps. In Death on Iona, each theory is examined in light of the surrounding history and facts. The narrative of Norah evolved into a quest for truth, and in the pursuit of an absolute, we may, in turn, discover God itself.

Death on Iona

The Curse of Osiris

Norah's father, Guiseppe Nicola Raimondo Fornario, also known as Joseph, harboured a deep love for Egypt, particularly Cairo, where he spent a significant portion of his time in the late 19th century. The city's monumental architecture, vibrant population, and millennia of rich history were merely the beginning of its allure for this passionate Northern African metropolis enthusiast.

Guiseppe found himself captivated by Cairo's past, which was shaped by the Fatimids, Mamluks, Ottomans, invasions, religious conflicts, and Pharaohs. He could only dream of leaving such a profound mark on history. Born in Naples, Italy, in 1863, Guiseppe swiftly discovered his calling in life and developed a passion for medicine.

He studied in Naples and Rome, becoming a highly respected figure in his field. His work on malaria research was only outshone by his love for travelling, which he did extensively. His father, Gerarde Fornario, had also been involved in medicine, and following in his footsteps was considered the proper path to take.

> *"What I hate is ignorance, smallness of imagination, the eye that sees no farther than its own lashes. All things are possible... Who you are is limited only by who you think you are."*

Egyptian Book of The Dead.

While moving between Italian and English universities and medical institutes, Guiseppe, in his late twenties, met the love of his life, Norah Edith Ling. In 1893, the couple, smitten with the idea of love and peace, married in the small suburb of Streatham, now part of the Borough of Lambeth, London.

It's worth noting that Streatham was in Surrey before becoming part of the County of London in 1889 and later, Greater London in 1965. Consequently, their marriage is recorded as having taken place in Surrey.

When 30-year-old Guiseppe wed 28-year-old Miss Ling, the ceremony was a modest affair, primarily attended by Miss Ling's family. Most of Guiseppe's relatives would have found the journey from Italy too challenging in the late 19th century.

Miss Ling was born in Manchester in 1865 to a prosperous retired tea merchant named Thomas Pratt Ling and his wife, Bristol-born Emily Ada Turner, who was also involved in the tea business. Thomas, born in Norwich, Norfolk, in 1836, came of age during the height of tea's adoption by the working class.

Previously, the beverage was primarily favoured by the upper class.

Today, when we purchase a box of teabags at the supermarket, we often forget the centuries of hard work and enterprise that have allowed us such convenience. Similar to the burgeoning internet industries of today, the tea business of the 19th century flourished.

Thomas's father had been involved in the tea trade, leaving the majority of his estate to Thomas. The Lings frequently travelled to India for business and to establish new contacts in what was one of the largest industries of the time. The couple were well-known in the tea trade and amassed considerable wealth, providing a life for their children where they would never have to struggle for food on the table.

Owing to their fortunate financial situation and social standing, Miss Ling and Guiseppe crossed paths, and before long, their lives were illuminated by the love they shared as the newly married Mr. and Mrs. Fornario. In 1897, four years after tying the knot and during one of their numerous trips to Egypt, Mrs. Fornario gave birth to a beautiful baby girl, with Guiseppe by her side.

They named their daughter Marie Edith Emily Norah Fornario. Her middle names were chosen in honour of her maternal lineage – Edith being her mother's middle name and Emily being her maternal grandmother's first name. Limited information exists about her father's ancestry beyond her paternal grandfather's name.

Norah, a common Italian name derived from Honora (or Honoria), can be traced back to the Latin word Honor, meaning honour. While some genealogy sites list her name as Nora, without the H, later census records and her death certificate show the spelling as Norah – as provided by her family and Norah herself to various officials over the years.

As we journey through this narrative together, we will discover that much has been distorted, inaccurately documented, and regrettably lost to the passage of time, such is the nature of a pre-digital era.

However, as is often the case with stories of true love, social class, and international travel in the 19th century, tragedy was bound to strike. In Hampshire, England, merely a year after their daughter's birth, Mrs. Fornario, suffering from severe complications during childbirth, succumbed to an illness before Norah's first birthday.

Mrs. Fornario, aged 33 in 1898, passed away, with her death recorded in the Christchurch registration district of the county. The fact that Norah would ultimately meet her end at the same age as her mother presents an eerie coincidence or destiny that has not escaped this researcher's attention.

Upon losing his wife at the age of 35, a heartbroken Guiseppe had to persevere with his medical research, leaving young Norah in the care of her grandparents,

Thomas and Emily. A few months after his wife's passing, Guiseppe returned to Egypt and eventually settled back in Italy.

Though he spent most of his time in Italy, he occasionally travelled to England to visit his in-laws and daughter. Guiseppe never remarried and had no other children, leaving Norah as the sole continuation of his lineage.

Norah's mother had two brothers, George Duncan Ling, born in Manchester in 1867, and Bertram Ling, born in 1875. At the time of their sister's death, George and Bertram were 31 and 23 years old, respectively.

In 1896, George married Florence Hannah Barnard and settled in an opulent home in Reigate, Surrey. Although little is documented about his life, it is believed that he might have been one of the countless victims of the First World War, leaving no trace of any offspring.

In 1902, when Bertram turned 27, he wed Florence Margaret Trapp and together they had three children. The fates of their twin sons remain shrouded in mystery, locked away in the annals of time, absent from historical records.

Their firstborn, Thomas Mortimer Ling, lived until 1973, ultimately passing away on the sun-kissed shores of Perth, Australia. The Ling and Fornario families were undeniably adventurous travellers during an era when international tourism was a luxury reserved for the select few who could afford it.

Death on Iona

> *"They are retained now, as are others, to the eternal corridors of time, right at the very edge of the expanding Universe where souls cross on their newest lines, waiting for the next star. They had become the starlight in the night sky as God had always intended."*
>
> Mentacracy.

In these modern times, it is astonishing how the past century's history can vanish into an abyss so deep that very little remains of those who once lived. It is known that in 1901, when Norah Fornario was merely four years old, she resided with her grandparents, Thomas and Emily, as well as her uncle Bertram.

They occupied an impressive estate called Leigham Holme in Streatham, along with three servants. Matilda Slapp, the 24-year-old parlour maid, Florence Heudson, the 30-year-old cook, and Jane Cole, the 29-year-old governess responsible for Norah's care when the Lings attended to business.

Having outlived their own daughter, Thomas and Emily likely viewed Norah as their own, raising her nearly from birth. Together, they forged a path for Norah that circumvented the typical struggles faced by working-class families, offering her something many children in the waning days of Victorian England desperately desired—a future.

Death on Iona

From 1902 onwards, Bertram, Norah's uncle, was seldom present in Streatham. He had moved out with his new wife and was preoccupied with travelling the country in his role as a director of public services. Streatham remained Norah's home, where she received her education, until tragedy would once again strike during her formative years. Perhaps this was a harbinger of her own impending fate.

But that other thing called death,

Which crumbles us up into good rich soil,

And sprouts grass, over the place

Or weeds -

What kind adjustment

That trues one nicely to the universe,

And bestows the good gift: the immortal insignificance

Of a leaf, or a grass blade,

Or one of the small stars!

Death by Viola I. Paradise.

Emily Ling outlived her daughter by a decade before succumbing to death on the 18th of February 1908. Aged 67, her passing was registered in Dorking, Surrey, a mere 19 miles from her residence. Her demise was natural, the result of a life spent navigating Victorian England and transitioning into the enigmatic industrialism of the 20th century.

For 11-year-old Norah, losing her grandmother felt like losing her mother once more. It is said that when first confronted with the grief of losing a close family member, one should acknowledge that this will not be the final instance of sorrow affecting the soul.

How Norah grieved remains uncertain, but death proved relentless, striking again just a year and a day after her grandmother's departure. Norah's grandfather, Thomas, succumbed to a heart attack brought on by old age and the stress of losing his daughter and wife. He died in his hometown of Norwich on the 19th of February 1909, aged 74.

By the time she turned 12, Norah had lost her mother and grandparents. She never knew her father's parents, as both had passed between Guiseppe's marriage to the love of his life and Norah's birth. Childhood encompasses not only the formative years, but also the opinions we inherit from our parents or acquire from others, which we carry into adulthood. Grief is an intense psychological anguish that can infiltrate the physical body, exacerbated by feelings of guilt and confusion.

At the tender age of 12, having already experienced immense loss, Norah found herself adrift in a world she had once endured. It seemed that death rarely left her life. It was hardly surprising that she would eventually seek solace in the unconventional, searching for answers where her family's foundation had failed her.

> *"All true growth and healing is from within outwards, therefore those who would minister to another's psychological need must learn to do so from the innermost sphere where all life is realised as one in essence, though manifesting outwardly in diversity of myriad forms."*
>
> Norah Fornario.

A mere two months following Thomas's passing, his solicitors attended to his will and estate. Thomas was comfortably wealthy, and his sons Bertram and George were already set to inherit the Ling tea dynasty.

Consequently, it aroused intrigue when Thomas bequeathed his entire fortune and savings to one individual: Norah. The notice of execution for his estate was published in numerous gazettes and newspapers throughout England and Wales, as required by law. On 16th April 1909, it read:

The will has been proved of Mr. Thomas Pratt Ling, of Bracondale, Dorking, Surrey, aged seventy-four, tea merchant, who died in February. He left £12,000 upon trust for his granddaughter Marie Nora Emily Edith Fornatio [sic], "provided that she shall remain under the guardianship of his son George or other person approved buy his trustees and shall not forsake the English Protestant Faith, or marry a person not of that Faith, or marry a first cousin on either her father's or her mother's side, under penalty of losing one-half of her interest in this sum, and he also provided that the income should be paid to her in the United Kingdom, unless for a cause to be certified by medical certificate, or other cause to be approved by his trustees, she shall not be in the United Kingdom.

Norah's surname is recorded as Fornatio, rather than Fornario, and there are several instances where the Fornario name was misspelled on both official and unofficial documents. Other variations include Formaris and Fonario. Some genealogical records list her name as Formaris, where the 'o' at the end of Fornario was mistaken for an 's', and the 'n' was interpreted as an 'm'.

The will was left to Norah 'upon trust', which meant she could access it upon turning 18. The conditions of the notice may appear peculiar at first, but they were relatively common during that era. The stipulation that Norah should not abandon the English Protestant faith or marry someone outside of that religion was one of many ways families could preserve their ancestors' religious lineage beyond death. After all, the Lings were a devoutly religious family.

Death on Iona

The requirement for Norah to remain in the United Kingdom to gain access to her trust was unsurprising. Her closest living relative was her father Guiseppe, who would only return to England out of necessity, as the country would have reminded him of his cherished wife's untimely death. As the years went by, Norah's relationship with her father improved, but she first had to navigate her turbulent teenage years.

Norah's uncle, George – mentioned in the will – and his spouse Florence resided in Reigate and welcomed Norah into their home following Thomas's death. It remains uncertain whether the will's details had left George feeling slighted and hurt, but he managed to oversee the Ling tea business for several years until his own demise sometime later.

The earnings from the tea empire must have been substantial, likely offsetting any trust bequeathed to Norah. Indeed, this is probably why Thomas left Norah his monetary savings and bonds, as he had already passed the significantly more valuable empire down to his two sons.

By the time the Second World War arrived, the tea industry had expanded immensely, with smaller tea merchants like the Ling enterprise being consumed by the colossal conglomerates that dominate the sector today. However, for a period, the Lings held a firm position within the tea business.

Their residence in Reigate, named Trenton, was situated on The Way, a street now lined with multimillion-pound homes. While George and his wife were far from struggling, even employing two servants, they were nonetheless obligated to take in 12-year-old Norah until she could access her estate.

Thomas bequeathed Norah a trust of £12,000 (GBP) in 1909, an astonishing sum for that era. This amount would be equivalent to approximately £1.5 million in 2023, with a cumulative price increase of over 12,500% due to an average annual inflation rate of 4.39% between 1909 and today. This £12,000 nest egg provided ample motivation for Norah to adhere to the terms of the notice.

In 1910, a year following her grandfather's death and four years before war erupted across Europe, 13-year-old Norah was enrolled by George in a school on England's South coast. The quaint Victorian town of Eastbourne would be her residence for the next few years. Norah attended the Ladies College, located at 2 Grassington Road, where her passion for writing blossomed and she found herself in the company of illustrious peers.

A mere stone's throw away on Summerdown Road stood St Cyprian's preparatory school for boys, a renowned institution that fostered a plethora of famed writers and intellectuals. Nestled between the Ladies College and St Cyprian's lay Compton Park, which has since been transformed into a golf course. During Eastbourne's balmy Summer days, lounging in the park would have been a favoured leisure activity for aspiring

Death on Iona

writers and dreamers, seeking inspiration from the vast sky above.

During Norah's time at the Ladies College, St Cyprian's was home to a young, eight-year-old George Orwell, who enrolled the same year Norah appeared in the census. While it would have been unusual for a 13-year-old girl to mingle with younger schoolboys, it is still a possibility. Chances are, she may have interacted with the future leaders and esteemed British military figures that St Cyprian's was renowned for producing.

Many Victorian-era schools and colleges in England had a relatively short lifespan, often being absorbed by larger educational institutions or repurposed as housing. The Ladies College, which operated from 1871 to 1920, was primarily led by long-serving Principal Marguerite Des Ruelles, who passed away in 1914, leaving an estate valued at £11,359.

In 1920, the Ladies College was transformed into the boys' boarding school Pennell House, which was eventually sold to housing developers in 1986. Today, a portion of Eastbourne College is named Pennell, as a tribute to the original Pennell school and, indirectly, the Ladies College.

Thanks to the diligent efforts of the Eastbourne Local History Society, a rare photograph of the Ladies College's students from a specific year was discovered. In the centre of the group of girls stands Principal Des Ruelles, whose final year at the college's helm was 1911

– coincidentally, the same year Norah is recorded in the census.

I managed to locate descendants of Des Ruelles who granted permission to print the following photograph, yet none could identify the pupils captured in the image, nor did they possess any additional photographs of the school's students.

Pupils of Ladies College, Eastbourne. Shared by Des Ruelles family.
Norah is likely pictured on the bottom right, dressed in black.

By a stroke of extraordinary luck, a photograph from that era exists, albeit grainy and undated. Principal Des Ruelles, seated in the centre and clad in black, appears to have aged in the picture, suggesting it may be from around 1911, if not precisely that year.

Ascertaining whether Norah is present in the image proves challenging; being half-Italian and half-English does not yield the exotic appearance one might expect, given that both heritages stem from European roots, albeit a blend of Northern and Mediterranean origins.

Among the young girls captured in the photograph, it is conceivable that one of them is Norah Fornario, aged between 13 and 15. Using AI and facial recognition technology, it seems likely that the girl at the bottom right, dressed in black, is a young Norah.

In various online discussions, blog posts, and articles chronicling her death, an accompanying photograph depicts a woman with a striking visage, dishevelled hair, and a somewhat 'new-age' aesthetic. This image has long been mistaken for Norah; however, it is actually a portrait of Moina Mathers, wife of Samuel Liddell Mathers, one of the founders of the Hermetic Order of the Golden Dawn.

The photo that has accompanied the stories has perpetuated the mystery via Chinese whispers and misinformation for over thirty years.

"If the lower nature is content to follow where the higher principles lead, it can be regenerated without suffering much of the pain entailed by its endeavour to drag down the soul; but a refusal to be regenerated necessitates its sacrifice that the soul may be liberated."

Norah Fornario.

Death on Iona

Photo of Moina Mathers, incorrectly cited as photo of Norah Fornario.

The image on the next page is of Norah Fornario, from a newspaper report released mere days after the incident. It is one of, if not the only photo of an adult Norah known to exist.

Photo of Norah Fornario, circa 1929.

The release of various census data over the years corroborates already existing data, such as electoral rolls, birth and death certificates, telephone directories, and trade directories. The significant societal shifts of that era render the 1921 census almost unrecognisable, even as recently as 1951.

However, the First World War took its toll on the electoral roll. The British Library possesses the national collection of printed electoral registers, ranging from their inception under the Representation of the People Act 1832 to the present day.

Although the Library's collection is complete for England, Wales, Scotland, and Northern Ireland from 1947 onwards, gaps exist prior to the Second World War. Registers were not published during the latter years of the First World War (1916–1917) or the Second World War (1940–1944). Consequently, the years between the two wars saw a considerable loss of information, rendering the register details between 1916 and 1947 rather sparse.

Venturing into the depths of Italian archives, which boast superior organisation compared to the UK's, I discovered details about the death of Norah's father, who outlived his daughter by 33 years—an eerie coincidence considering the number 33. Norah passed away at 33, her mother died at the same age, and her father survived 33 years longer than his child.

His death, seldom discussed, involved a cardinal from Boston, USA. As documented in the 1950 Boston Record, Francis Cardinal Spellman and 300 American Roman Catholic Holy Year Pilgrims arrived in Nice, France, travelling from Rome, Italy.

This intriguing connection between Norah's father's passing and the cardinal's visit to France adds another layer of complexity to the family's already enigmatic history. It is these puzzling connections and unforeseen discoveries that make delving into the past both fascinating and bewildering, as the truth often lies shrouded in a web of coincidences and hidden details.

Death on Iona

In Rome, Cardinal Spellman ventured beyond the Archdiocese Palace to visit a sightless physician residing in a flat on the city's outskirts—a man who had once saved his life. This individual was none other than Guiseppe Fornario, Norah's father. In 1911, Spellman chose to pursue the priesthood, and Archbishop William Henry O'Connell dispatched him to study at the Pontifical North American College in Rome.

During his time in Rome, Spellman fell ill with pneumonia, and his health deteriorated to such an extent that the seminary administration considered returning him to the United States. In 1914, he found himself admitted to a medical institution where Guiseppe was employed as a doctor. Over the course of five months, Guiseppe cared for Spellman, ultimately nursing him back to health.

Spellman remained in Rome, finishing his theological studies. He was ordained as a priest by Patriarch Ceppetelli on 14th May 1916 and journeyed back to the U.S. soon after. In 1950, the cardinal paid a 20-minute visit to Guiseppe's home, where the two engaged in a heartfelt conversation, the contents of which have remained undisclosed. As the cardinal prepared to depart, Guiseppe presented him with a bronze statue as a memento.

Guiseppe passed away on 5th January 1953, aged 89, with Cardinal Spellman following not long after. The statue given to the cardinal is of particular interest, as Guiseppe, despite adhering to Christian beliefs, accepted Egyptian myth and magic as truth. He bestowed upon Spellman a statue of Osiris, the god of the underworld—a similar statue he had gifted Norah a year before her death, much to her chagrin due to her father's beliefs.

A 1930 interview, sourced from Italian records, with Guiseppe was published in the Milwaukee Sentinel, just four months after Norah's demise. The article, headlined "Weird Death of Scientist's Daughter Linked With Cursed Statue," delved into the mysterious circumstances surrounding Norah's passing and the enigmatic statue, leaving readers to ponder the eerie connections between these seemingly unrelated events.

Dr. Joseph [*Guiseppe*] Fornario, director of the Medical Institute at Milan, Italy, is one of the country's most eminent scientists. He did not believe in spiritualism, mental telepathy and the mysteries of the occult in which his daughter, the late Nora Emil [sic] Fornario, was so intensely interested. But since the girl's mysterious and sudden death, he is ready to admit there may be something in her theories - something that cannot be analyzed in the test tubes and under the eye of the microscope in the laboratory.

Milwaukee Sentinel, 9th March 1930.

In the year 1928, Norah embarked on a documented journey to Egypt with her father, which would be the last time he would see his daughter alive. Desiring to provide his only child with a meaningful keepsake from their travels, he purchased an ancient statue of the god Osiris for her. The Milwaukee Sentinel reported a conversation that allegedly occurred after Norah had implored her father not to acquire the statue.

'To me, Osiris is the symbol of tragedy and violent death. If you remember your Egyptian mythology, Osiris was murdered and his spirit became the Judge of the Dead. I'm sure the statue would bring me all kinds of bad luck.'

'Don't be silly Norah, Osiris was the god of light and health and virtue. I insist that you get over your absurd notions and do me the honour of accepting my gift.'

It is claimed that an argument occurred in the daylight of the markets but Norah gave into her father's wishes, but "she warned him that he had forced her to become the possessor of an omen of evil, and that if anything happened to her he would only have himself to blame."

The sentinel story continued:

"By the time Nora was ready to leave on her visit to Ionia [sic], "the curse of Osiris" had become her father's pet joke, for his daughter had continued to enjoy the best of health. But the girl could not share his humour concerning a superstition that went deep into her nature. She had been living on Ionia only a few months when the family with whom she was staying went to her sleeping room one morning and discovered that the young woman had not slept in her bed.

Death on Iona

A thorough search of the premises was made, and then the alarmed hosts set out along a lonely path which led to a bleak headland, where Nora spent much of her time reading books on the occult and meditating about the psychic phenomena in which she so intensely believed. And there they found her body, and in her lifeless hand a book opened to a chapter on the myths built around Osiris. There was no evidence of suicide, but the expression on the young woman's face indicated that she had died with her staring eyes focused on some terrifying object, or vision."

The Milwaukee Sentinel, notorious for publishing errors during that era, should not be regarded as a reliable source for the original Italian account, particularly as the tale appears amidst a collection of children's myths. I must clarify that no statue of Osiris was discovered clutched in Norah's lifeless hands, nor was there any book open to a page discussing Osiris, or any book at all, for that matter.

The presence of the Osiris statue at the death scene is one of many falsehoods that have persisted and multiplied over the years. Additionally, Iona was never referred to as Ionia, which was, in reality, an ancient region situated along the central portion of the western coast of Anatolia in present-day Turkey.

In an article titled The Strange Death of Norah Fornario, author Elizabeth Melville described how Guiseppe was overwhelmed by an eerie sense of dread and doom two days prior to the discovery of Norah's body. The article suggests that Guiseppe attributed these feelings to a premonition or telepathy, implying that he never forgave himself for giving her the Osiris statue.

The fact that he also gifted the same statue to Bishop Stillman remains perplexing, especially if he ultimately believed the curse of Osiris was responsible for his daughter's demise. The notion of telepathy first emerged in a report on 5th December 1929 from the Scotsman, translated from an interview in an Italian newspaper.

"He was unable to account for his fears yet could not shake off the feeling that something was wrong. Two days later a telegram arrived announcing that the dead body of his daughter had just been discovered."

Aside from the article, no other newspaper pieces or records mention Guiseppe experiencing any premonitions prior to Norah's death. Nevertheless, it is plausible that the connection between a parent and their child can lead to inexplicable occurrences. We shall delve deeper into the psychic aspect of Norah's death later in the book.

Upon completing her education, Norah briefly resided with her uncle and aunt, with whom it was rumoured she had a strained relationship. When Norah turned 18, she accessed her grandfather's trust and purchased a property on Mortlake Road in Kew, London – a considerable expense, even during the 1910s.

On 4th July 1922, Marie Edith Emily Nora Fornario received her nationality and naturalisation certificate, becoming an official UK citizen. In the early 20th century, obtaining citizenship through naturalisation or denization was a costly and intricate process, typically only pursued by the affluent and well-connected.

As a result, only a small fraction of immigrants to England would have formally acquired citizenship. Norah's naturalisation certificate, numbered A9304, confirmed her Italian origins. With her English mother and grandparents deceased and her father Italian, her nationality was listed as Italian, dispelling some online speculations that she was Egyptian.

The 1844 Naturalisation Act stipulated that every foreigner seeking residence in Britain must provide specific information and take an oath of allegiance and supremacy. Subsequently, a certificate granting permission to remain in the country would be issued. A newly naturalised individual would retrospectively acquire all citizen rights from their birth.

Naturalisation certificates were announced and published in the London, Edinburgh, or Belfast Gazette. Records created after 1922 remained closed for a century unless a review was requested at the national archives. Norah's record, however, was established shortly before the new legislation took effect and has been accessible since 1995.

Around the time Norah obtained British citizenship, she became involved in something that would ultimately lead her to her untimely end.

The Voices of the Elemental Kingdoms

While in Hastings, I discovered the works of Aleister Crowley, but I wasn't completely enthralled, as many of the 20th century occultists built on the foundations of what had come before. Yet, it was through Crowley I learned of the Hermetic Order of the Golden Dawn, its spin-off groups, and other occultists of the time, including Dion Fortune.

Through Dion Fortune, I discovered a murder mystery regarding a half-Italian female named Miss Fornario. My own life at that time was spent seeking answers to questions I did not expect an answer to, my fears of loneliness and of the great beyond mirrored the feelings of my peers and the people around me. It remains unclear if anyone truly escapes the fear of loneliness, for a darkness can persist throughout the corridors of time and amidst the lines that connect our lives.

As such, it was unfortunate I had met Norah at such a time, though had the times not been such then we would not have met. Regrettable because that was over twenty years ago and her story has propagated with such falsehoods, that in some fashion, I feel responsible for not having delved deeper and setting the record straight sooner.

Among those who have never taken the time to understand the true meaning of the occult, they are bombarded with images from horror movies, books, and media, stating as a matter of fact that to be involved in the occult is to be involved with the devil. The truth couldn't be much further away.

It is with great irony that many of those who misunderstand the occult, do at the same time take solace in reading their star signs, holding a gemstone nearby, lighting incense, using candles for a loved one, or visiting fortune-tellers to have their palms read – all traditional occult practices.

The occult is generally acknowledged to involve practices that fall on the edge of science and mainstream religion, which may involve phenomena appearing to invoke fear. The truth is, as I quickly discovered, the occult, at its heart, is mostly about seeking answers to questions regarding life, the Universe, our own planet, and how we coexist with nature. It can be taken further to include understanding how our own minds work and how best to focus our energy on a mental state.

Fundamentally, the occult is the search for knowledge. If a foundation of knowledge can be learned, understood, and utilised, then that knowledge can be spread far and wide. From the late 19th century to the early 20th and up to the Second World War, occultism had found a foothold in Great Britain, as it had done across the western world.

My first encounter with Norah was through Dion Fortune in one of her many books entitled Psychic Self-Defense. Published in the Summer of 1930, Dion quotes a story found in the January 1930 edition of The Occult Review.

It's important to note that this is taken verbatim from the Occult Review and not written by Dion herself. The Occult Review was a publication dedicated to following the occult renaissance of the early 20th and promoting essays and articles by notable and upcoming authors and thinkers, including Norah, as we'll discover later.

The mysterious death of a student of occultism, Miss N. Fornario, is receiving the attention of the authorities at the present time. Miss Fornario was found lying nude on the bleak hill-side in the lonely island of Iona. Round her neck was a cross secured by a silver chain, and near at hand lay a large knife which had been used to cut a large cross in the turf. On this cross her body was lying.

A resident of London, Miss Fornario seems to have made her way to Iona for some purpose connected with occultism. One of the servants at her house in London stated that a letter had been received saying she had a 'terrible case of healing on'.

One newspaper report alludes to 'mysterious stories on the island about blue lights having been seen in the vicinity of where her body was found, and there is also a story of a cloaked man'. Occultists no less than the general public will await with interest any disclosures that may be forthcoming concerning this occurrence."

The Occult Review January 1930.

Dion continues her piece on Norah, with an unusual point and something that perhaps instigated a lot of the mystery surrounding Norah's death. For when a great thinker of the time, who is still considered a great thinker, writes about something she knew that no one else did then a reaction would have been expected.

"No disclosures ever were forthcoming, however, and conjecture alone can work upon the case. One detail only can I add to the brief but comprehensive report of the Occult Review. The body bore marks of scratches."

Unless Dion was privy to having witnessed the body of Norah on Iona or had access to an autopsy, of which there was none, then there is no possible way Dion would have known about any scratches on the body. It could have been assumed that because Norah was found nude near rocks, her body may well have borne scratches or marks of some kind. It seems to me that a logical conclusion could have been made.

Death on Iona

To understand Dion's writings about Norah, we have to look at the context of the book in which it was written. 'Psychic Self Defense' is a detailed instruction manual on protecting oneself from a paranormal attack. It explains how to recognise the signs of a psychic haunting and overcome its physical aspects and understand the methods and motives behind such an attack.

Dion believed that victims of astral attacks always bore scratch marks, and to bring Norah's story into her work, she might have wanted to embellish the death ever so slightly. Some news reports at the time mention scratches on Norah's feet, but none mention marks on her body. Dion goes on to form her own opinion and a brief history of her relationship with Norah.

"I knew Miss Fornario intimately, and at one time we did a good deal of work together, but some three years before her death we went our separate ways and lost sight of each other. She was half Italian and half English, of unusual intellectual calibre, and was especially interested in the Green Ray elemental contacts; too much interested in them for my peace of mind, and I became nervous and refused to co-operate with her.

"I do not object to reasonable risks, in fact one cannot expect to achieve anything worthwhile in life if one will not take risks, but it appeared to me that "Mac," as we called her, was going into very deep waters, even when I knew her, and that there was certain to be trouble sooner or later. She had evidently been on an astral expedition from which she never returned. She was not a good subject for such experiments, for she suffered from some defect of the pituitary body.

"Whether she was the victim of a psychic attack, whether she merely stopped out on the astral too long and her body, of poor vitality in any case, became chilled lying thus exposed in mid-winter, or whether she slipped into one of the elemental kingdoms that she loved, even as Swinburne swam out to sea, who shall say? The information at our disposal is insufficient for an opinion to be formed. The facts, however, cannot be questioned, and remain to give sceptics food for thought."

Although there is no written record of when and where the two had met, according to Dion, they parted ways in 1926. It appears, if we are to read into Dion's writings, although laced with inconsistencies, that Dion herself was becoming 'nervous' of Norah's path and ultimately 'refused to co-operate with her'.

Which is unusual as Norah was not doing anything beyond the realms of occultism that would have inspired others to turn against her. Perhaps then, it was Norah's own fascination and dedication to one particular aspect of occultism that separated her from her peers.

In her teens, according to her father's later report, Norah had spent a lot of time in Italy as an Italian citizen, though any documentation regarding her time there is not recorded and simply does not exist. When she turned 18 in 1915, she was able to access her trust fund and begin the process of purchasing a property.

From the age of 18 to 25, Norah began to involve herself in the occult and met Dion around that time.

That Dion knew Norah intimately is something to note, as Norah is not known to have had any relationships with anyone throughout her life, at least not extended ones. She would have been a teenager in Italy, and a carefree one at that, and it is impossible to say if she had been with someone there or not.

Italian press did not write about the case until many decades after her father's death. By that point, the story had become so distorted that even Norah's name was misspelled. Finding anyone who may have had a relationship with Norah in Italy would prove impossible.

Dion was known for her strong, magnetic personality, but was not carefree. According to Alan Richardson's 2007 book 'Priestess: The Life and Magic of Dion Fortune', there were rumours that she had sexual relationships with both men and women, but there is no solid evidence to support this.

It's possible that Dion and Norah were intimately acquainted, but we have no evidence to confirm this. Dion's choice of language in her book and the theories of other authors suggest that they may have been close. It seems abrupt that Dion would refuse to cooperate with Norah after working together for so many years.

That Dion referred to her as 'Mac' is also important as one of Norah's pseudonyms was Mac Tyler, who Norah published some of her works under. Now, sadly lost to time, only one Mac Tyler piece exists, entitled 'The Use of Imagination in Art, Science and Business', and published in Occult Review volume 48, number 1, in July 1928, now out of copyright and found in the appendices of this book.

Members of the Hermetic Order of the Golden Dawn and the Alpha et Omega group chose mottoes as pseudonyms, which they used to refer to each other. Higher-ranking members often chose foreign or aspirational names, while members on the fringes, like Norah, could choose names that contained high-minded sentiments or literary allusions.

Norah chose 'Mac' as her motto, possibly because she was fascinated with The Immortal Hour, a play by Scottish playwright Fiona Macleod (a pseudonym of writer William Sharp). It's unclear why she chose 'Tyler' as a surname, as there is no apparent link to her interests or ideals.

> *"The artist's imaginative faculty is frequently in need of training and discipline, for unless it is balanced by clear reason, it is apt to distort the spiritual truths it strives to express, instead of embodying them in beautiful and helpful form."*
>
> Norah Fornario.

In the late 1910s, Dion associated herself with occultist and Freemason Theodore Moriarty, who ran a Masonic-influenced lodge in Hammersmith, London. Moriarty was friends with Arthur Conan Doyle, who was interested in joining Freemasonry and the Golden Dawn, of which Moriarty was associated.

Though there is no real-world evidence to link any real person to the creation of Doyle's Sherlock Holmes nemesis, Professor Moriarty, the connection to Theodore remains, especially as he refused to sponsor Doyle's transition to Freemasonry, inciting a bit of a spat between the two. Dion also immortalised him in her own fiction as Dr. Taverner.

Moriarty had left traditional freemasonry in 1907, with his resignation listed from the St Blaize Lodge, Mossel Bay No. 1938, in South Africa. With his beliefs in occultism, he set about creating one of the first co-masonic freemasonry groups, in Sinclair Road, Hammersmith, that allowed females to be initiated.

From there, he grew a community at the home of Gwen Stafford-Allen in Bishop's Stortford, Herefordshire. Gwen was the daughter of Francis Allen, who lived at the giant Cockley Cley estate in Norfolk, close to where Norah's grandfather was born and had lived.

It was at this community where Dion became a follower of Moriarty's work and would go on to cite him as her true teacher. The community, that Moriarty called the 'Science, Arts and Crafts Society', was an occult group that overlapped teachings of Masonry, Theosophy, and the Hermetic Order of the Golden Dawn.

In 1920, Norah was initiated into Moriarty's co-masonic lodge and is there she would have met Dion, though they may also have met at the meetings of the Science, Arts and Crafts Society, where it was likely she was invited to the lodge.

Norah's name is listed in the officer records for the 1920/1921 years. She is named as Outer Guardian of the co-masonic lodge. By proxy, Norah would find herself at the heart of the occult wars that propagated through the 1920s.

Dion soon left the lodge to involve herself in the Golden Dawn, which had suffered as a result of the First World War, its founder Samuel Liddell MacGregor Mathers had died of the flu epidemic in 1918. The Golden Dawn was then taken over by his wife, Moina Mathers. In August 1923, Moriarty died, and Fortune was touted as the new leader of the Science, Arts and Crafts Society but was usurped by Stafford-Allen.

It's strange when we talk about early 20th century occultism, that one group stands far above the rest. That being the Golden Dawn, but the truth is that the Golden Dawn, as it was birthed in 1887, only lasted the sum of 16 years before its dissolution in 1903. A few years earlier in 1899, there was a war brewing among adepts of the Golden Dawn. Some members had come to despise Mather's leadership and his close friendship with a student of the occult named Aleister Crowley.

From then until 1903, splinter groups had broken away from the main Golden Dawn and formed their own temples. At around the same time, Mathers, empowered by those remaining loyal to his leadership, renamed the Golden Dawn as the Rosicrucian Order of Alpha et Omega, more commonly known as Alpha et Omega, or AO.

This is why when we talk about this period of occultism, the Alpha et Omega was the Golden Dawn, just renamed to usher in a new era. But that new era died with Mathers in 1918, and it was left to Moina to carry on and re-establish. Dion was initiated into Alpha et Omega in 1919 but later said:

> *"When I came in touch with his organisation, it was manned mainly by widows and grey-bearded ancients and did not appear to be a very promising field of occult endeavour. But I had considerable experience of practical occultism before I made its acquaintance, and I immediately recognised power of a degree and kind I had never met before and had not the slightest doubt but that I was on the trail of the genuine tradition, despite its inadequate exposition."*
>
> Dion Fortune.

At some point between 1921 and 1922, Norah became a member of the Alpha et Omega group, with the encouragement of both Fortune and Mathers. There, she was able to develop her own psychic abilities of faith-healing and telepathy, and became close with both powerful women, who at times struggled to get along.

In 1924, Dion formed her own occult group with Glastonbury-based friend Charles Loveday, and together they developed The Society of Inner Light, based on elements of theosophy. Though the group had no relation to the Golden Dawn, Mathers was aggrieved at Fortune, not only for taking lead of a new occult group, but for a number of articles in The Occult Review that suggested readers should be concerned about the path that Mathers was taking the Alpha et Omega group down.

Mathers expelled Fortune from the AO and claimed it was due to Fortune having the wrong signs in her aura. Norah found herself stuck between wanting to study more of the occult, and the two women who she had befriended and come to hold in high esteem. She split from the AO and followed Fortune for a little while longer, which in turn was said to have angered Mathers further.

It's important to talk about Mathers and Fortune, as many writers believe Mathers was able to psychically attack and kill Norah from beyond the grave, and the troubles between occult groups may have been the cause for that.

In late 1924, The Society of Inner Light founded its base at 3 Queensborough Terrace, Bayswater, London, to use as a temple and headquarters. In 1925, Norah was one of the first initiates, and stayed with the group until 1926 when Norah continued down a path that concerned Fortune.

On the Pentecost, Sunday 23rd May 1926, the society held a spiritual ritual at an old orchard they had purchased at the foot of Glastonbury Tor. There, it was recorded they all underwent a spiritual experience so powerful that the members were left with a feeling of ecstasy running through them, a sensation that a great power was nearby. Norah was with them and believed that the experience was a direct result of a messenger from the elemental kingdoms.

Although it influenced the society's beliefs going forward, Norah began to focus on the elemental kingdom itself. Using Dion's own words from above, Norah *'was especially interested in the Green Ray elemental contacts; too much interested in them for my peace of mind, and I became nervous and refused to co-operate with her.'*

Norah then tumbled down a rabbit hole so overwhelming and powerful, that the search for the elementals would ultimately take her to the Scottish island of Iona, which resulted in her mysterious death.

Death on Iona

The Age of Influence

By the end of 1926, aged 29, Norah found herself separated from any allegiances she had. She was no longer a member of any secret group or occult order, and instead forged her own path through occult writings and thoughts. She had the security of a large property in London, paid for with her trust fund, and a desire to learn more about the mysterious elementals.

Why then was Fortune, a powerful occultist in her own right, so nervous about Norah's interest in a field that Fortune sometimes wrote about?

> *'She had evidently been on an astral expedition from which she never returned.'*

Why did Fortune outright refuse to work with Norah any longer? It could be that Fortune saw deteriorating mental health in Norah and refused on the basis she didn't want Norah learning more in order to help her health – rather than simply abandoning her friend.

Regarding astral expeditions and rituals, Dion said that Norah *'was not a good subject for such experiments, for she suffered from some defect of the pituitary body.'* A pituitary gland is a small pea-sized gland that plays a major role in regulating vital body functions and general wellbeing. It can also be responsible for vision problems, headaches, and dizziness.

It is possible that in the line above, Fortune was referring to Norah's mental health. The only other possibility is that Norah had a tumour on the pituitary gland that would have caused growths, resulting in bodily defects. There is no evidence to suggest Norah had a tumour, and so the defect Fortune mentions could well have been to do with psychological health.

Without the strength of occult groups to guide her, Norah continued studying and exploring the occult by herself, which in many circles, is dangerous in itself.

> *"I warn all of you, never, never, never. You'll not only lose your mind, you'll lose your soul."*
>
> Christopher Lee, 2011.

Norah developed a fascination with the concept of the elementals, which are mythic beings often discussed in occult literature and have been recorded in written form since the 16th century works of Swiss alchemist

Paracelsus. These entities range from fairies to gnomes and correspond to the ancient elements of earth, water, air, and fire.

Norah's particular interest was in the Green Ray Elementals, associated with one of the three paths outlined in the doctrine of The Society of Inner Light. However, elements of the Green Rays also correspond with Alpha et Omega and formed the foundation of her research into the occult.

According to the teachings of the inner light (abbreviated):

On the Green Ray, man seeks God in Nature and worships Him there.

Achieving that Divine Ecstasy is the method and discipline of the Way of the Green Ray. And it is an inebriation of the soul, not of the flesh.

But this Path also has its dangers, for it tends to turn in upon itself and issue whence it came. It may become a fixed state and not a Path, and the soul lingering there may be overtaken by night.

There the Subconscious Self may worship the Old Gods and possibly escape from the synthesis which is man and become lost in a limbo of forgotten things to wander in obscurity.

The paths to God are many. Your need may be one thing and your desire another, say the Masters.

There's a phrase that always jumps out when I look at Norah's tale, 'escape from the synthesis which is man and become lost in a limbo of forgotten things.' For there has long been a theory that while Norah was on Iona, she connected with the Elemental Kingdom and thus became lost in the limbo between our world and the next.

To understand why Norah went to Iona and how she died, we first need to look at what influenced her to go there in the first place. Away from the occult world, Norah was heavily influenced by two people.

The first was Dundee-born artist John Duncan, born in 1866 to a hard-working butcher. By the age of 20, he was already working in London as a commercial illustrator and made most of his income from portraits. His passion, however, was Celtic mythology, legends, and more specifically: fairies.

It was reported that Duncan would hear faerie music while painting, and he believed them to be elementals from another realm. He took it upon himself to visualise the faerie realm through his art. He also spent a lot of time in Italy and became disappointed with representations of elementals across Europe. He aimed to reconnect those who viewed his paintings with a lost heritage he believed had been buried by other artists of his day.

His most famous painting was the 1911 work titled "The Riders of the Sídhe," which envisioned a parallel realm beneath the earth inhabited by Celtic Fae, known as the Sídhe or Aos Sí. Unlike the common European fairies, Celtic fae are tall and handsome, much like high elves.

Riders of the Sidhe by John Duncan, 1911.

The Aos Sí were defeated by the Milesians during the invasion of their land, resulting in the great battle of Tailltin. Eventually, they established a parallel realm beneath the earth and coexist invisibly with the world of humans. They are generally benign, unless angered.

The Sídhe are often portrayed as beautiful and magical, with the power to bestow blessings or curses upon humans. They are associated with nature, particularly with the land and the sea, and are often depicted as guardians of ancient knowledge and secrets. In some tales, they are also believed to be able to shapeshift and to control the weather.

Many trees and mounds, or sidhes fall under their protection, and should a mortal harm them, a curse is put upon him and his descendants. Home and roads are not built to cross the ley-lines, the underground fairy paths, lest strange things happen. When a host of the Sidhe pass by, you hear a strange sound, like the humming of a thousand bees.

Sídhe is the Irish word for mounds, Aos Sí translates as 'people of the mounds'. Iona is said to be home to one of these mounds, simply called the Fairy Mound or Fairy Hill. Duncan struggled throughout his life as his own family thought his works were ugly and not fit for public consumption.

Believing that he was capturing a lost world for future generations, he spent a lot of time on Iona from 1903, sometimes staying with the Camerons and other times at the St Columba Hotel. Iona became close to his heart, and he was once quoted as saying, '*Iona, dear and lovely as ever. Didn't paint, of course.*'

One of his masterpieces was the 1913 painting 'St. Bride'. It is a beautiful painting of a female dressed in a gown being carried by angels from Iona to Bethlehem. Duncan intended the painting to be a bridge between the Celts and Christianity, and the woman's removal from Iona was to illustrate the Celtic demise and entry into the new world.

St. Bride by John Duncan, 1913.

For someone like Norah, who had suffered many losses at such a young age and lost herself in the teachings of multiple occult orders, Duncan's paintings, and especially St. Bride, would have engrained itself on her soul.

Norah studied Duncan's works and life and discovered that he had travelled to Iona to use as a basis for his paintings. Due to the minimal amount of accommodation on Iona in the late 19th and early 20th

Century, it is a possibility that he may have stayed in the same lodgings as Norah had done before her death there.

It is with tragic hindsight that Duncan died alone in 1945, unhappy with his accomplishments, having lost his 'inner eye' and suffered immense criticism before the First World War. To some people, he was a madman consumed with the faerie realm, to others, like Norah, he was a visualiser of a world just out of reach. Although, he was one of the few artists who helped keep the faerie realm alive and is revered today.

The second greatest influence on Norah's life, apart from the occult, was the prolific writer William Sharp, who wrote under the pseudonym Fiona Macleod. His writings probably enticed Norah further since he was known to be an active member of the occult world in the late Victorian period, although he died in 1905, many years before Norah discovered him. Sharp was a member of the early incarnation of the Golden Dawn and would have been known to Moina Mathers, who initiated Norah into the Alpha et Omega.

Sharp's lasting legacy was the abundance of Faerie lore he left behind in the writings of Fiona Macleod, which led Norah to become an expert in analysing his works. It was not a coincidence that Sharp had spent time on Iona as a visitor on at least three occasions between 1884 and 1899, and he usually stayed at the St Columba Hotel.

Death on Iona

> *"There is another Iona than the Iona of sacred memories and prophecies; Iona the metropolis of dreams. None can understand it who does not see it through its pagan light, its Christian light, its singular blending of paganism and romance and spiritual beauty."*
>
> Fiona Macleod (William Sharp).

Although his body of work was extensive, there was one piece that Norah was drawn back to time and again. It was a play called *The Immortal Hour*, written in 1899. When the play ran at the Regents Theatre in London in 1923, it was noted that Norah sat in the audience 23 times, taking something new from the imagery and symbolism with each viewing.

This led her to write a short interpretation of the play, which was published as a small booklet by Frederick Newman in London later that year. The booklet is now out of copyright and reprinted in the appendices of this book.

> *"There is a fourth class who… sense the existence of a deeper meaning but are hopelessly baffled by their inability to interpret the intricate symbolism employed. It was for such seekers that this interpretation*

> *was written, and in the hope that these tentative suggestions, based on a study of comparative religion, folklore, mysticism and symbolism will provide them with the necessary clues."*

Norah Fornario, writing as Mac Tyler.

With Sharp's written works, Duncan's artistry, and teachings from the world of the occult, Norah was armed with a fascination of the elemental realm that far surpassed that of her peers at the time. Throughout human history, there have been a variety of false occultists proclaiming their way is the only way, imitators of a hidden knowledge scraped from those who have studied for the cause. Their purpose is to entrap those on their mission to the truth, with confusion and false hope.

Norah was an occultist who sought to transcend her isolation along with her own fears of a Godless world, a place where Satan could replace Jesus as King of earth. It was her isolation that allowed her passion to grow into an overbearing desire for truth. Amid the mystery of the elementals, she would soon leave her home in London and seek the answers she was looking for, in the one place that connected her peers, her friends, her influences, and the faerie kingdoms: Iona.

The Call of the Sacred Island

Iona's shorelines are vastly different from those of Hastings, and though I see the appeal of Iona, I much prefer the simple seaside town tropes of shingle beaches and biting tourist traps. While on a research trip for David Gemmell in Hastings, which turned into an Aleister Crowley crash course, I remember sitting on the shoreline with a friend.

Together, we looked out to the lands beyond the horizon, that country a lifetime away, and imagined the great demons and legends that held sway over the foreign lands. Then, when night fell, and the town disappeared under a veil of mist and dim streetlights, we looked up to the sky in the distance and imagined what wonders lay beyond the realm of the stars' canopy.

It was then I knew that even though I had touched on the story of Norah, I would one day find my way to Iona to see for myself what the attraction was and why so many had ventured there for a multitude of reasons.

Death on Iona

"We rarely leave the illusory safety of our home in the hills, these days, and I have no desire to take that route over the sea to Iona."

Molly Whittington-Egan, Scottish Murder Stories, 1998.

It turned out that it would be another 13 years before I took the boat from Mull to Iona in 2013 and stepped onto what had become a revered place in my own mind. Iona is known as the cradle of Christianity because it was the landing place of St. Columba, an Irish Christian missionary, in 563 AD.

He came to spread Christianity to Scotland and established a monastery on Iona, which became an important center of Celtic Christianity. From Iona, Columba and his followers went on to spread Christianity throughout Scotland and beyond, and the island became a place of pilgrimage for Christians. From 793 AD, the island was attacked in the Viking invasion of Scotland, but they didn't settle there, instead, allowing a small community of monks to live on the island.

Nothing remains of the 6th century monks led by St. Columba, but the Abbey built later by Benedictine monks in the 13th century does remain, after careful reconstruction in the early and mid-20th century. The smaller St Oran's Chapel dates from the early 12th century and around it were buried a number of West Highland clan chiefs. This area became the graveyard for the island's local population, in use for generations past and present.

Iona from the sea by Lynda B.

For Christian pilgrims and tourists, Iona is a powerful place, and many visit to pay their respects to Columba. For non-religious tourists, the island offers an insight to island living in Scotland, along with stunning landscapes, rugged shorelines, and a feeling of being at one with nature.

In the Summer, the guesthouses are full, and the ferry from Fionnphort on the island of Mull to Iona is jam-packed with day trippers and island hoppers. For the more adventurous – if you're willing to risk the windy waters around the islands – then a visit to Staffa from Iona or Fionnphort is a possibility on a good weather day.

Needless to say that Iona is a popular tourist destination, and with an average of 130 residents, the islanders go above and beyond to welcome their visitors, which number over 100,000 every single year. Some of these visitors, including myself in 2013, go there for reasons that many do not know about.

Norah is buried in the local cemetery that surrounds St Oran's Chapel. Most tourists who visit the island will have never heard the name of Norah Fornario, and many will pass by her unassuming gravestone without a second thought about who she was. But for those, like me, whose journey into the heart of the Fornario story takes us to the cradle of Christianity, we seek out the gravestone to remind ourselves that yes, she did exist, and her death was as mysterious as it was explainable.

There is a place on Iona known by two names: Sìthean Mòr or big hill of the fairies, as smooth green hills are often linked with fairy lore; and Cnoc nan Aingeal, hill of the Angels. Columba's biographer records that the saint would pray on top of the hill. One afternoon, shortly before dusk set in, a prying monk followed Columba to the hill and witnessed Columba in communion with the angels.

There, on top of the mound, there were said to be angels floating around Columba, clad in white garments and moving at great speeds. It was then that the legend of the Fairy Hill was born and remains one of Iona's most popular sites.

It is also said that Norah's nude body was found on top of Sìthean Mòr, in the exact place where Columba had held communion with the angels. As we get to that point in the story, we'll see that the reported discovery of Norah's body on the Mòr was not entirely accurate.

> *"Miss Fornario was something of an artist and one who (rightly) felt that Britain had gone wrong in the 7th Century in choosing, at the Synod of Whitby, to follow the Pauline Christianity of Rome rather than that of Columba in Iona."*
>
> Alan Richardson, Dion Fortune's Biographer.

But why did Columba choose Iona as his landing place and not somewhere more populated? Although many claim religious reasons, the truth was that Columba upset the king of Ireland by refusing to hand over an illegally copied Gospel, which led to a battle that Columba and his warrior family won. He fled the country and settled on the first place he found where he couldn't see Ireland over the waters, which turned out to be Iona.

Death on Iona

Some spiritualists believe that Columba went to Iona as the island has long been seen as a site where the veil between the elemental kingdom or Heaven was closer to our world than many other places. Though there is no evidence to suggest that Columba went to Iona for those reasons, the island is still seen as a place where the two worlds meet. Fourteen centuries after Columba's arrival, tales of Iona's location would echo in Norah's mind. She went to Iona not to flee war, but in the belief that Iona was a thin place.

Thin places are considered to be locations where the veil between the physical and spiritual worlds is believed to be particularly thin. Many such places are steeped in myth and legend and attract spiritual seekers and tourists alike.

Other well-known thin places include the Isle of Skye, also in Scotland, Glastonbury and Stonehenge in England, Rock of Cashel, Knock, and Cashelkilty Stone Circle in Ireland, and the Mojave Desert in California, Lourdes in France, and Aotearoa in New Zealand, where the faeries are known in Māori mythology as Patupaiarehe or Tūrehu. Each of these places offers unique spiritual experiences and connections to the mystical realm.

> *"It's a Celtic concept, one that stems from an old proverb that says, 'Heaven and earth are only three feet apart, but in the thin places that distance is even smaller.' In thin places,*

the folklore goes, the barrier between the physical world and the spiritual world wears thin and becomes porous. Invisible things, like music or love or dead people or God, might become visible there, or if they don't become visible they become so present and tangible that it doesn't matter. Distinctions between you and not-you, real and unreal, worldly and otherworldly, fall away."

Jordan Kisner, "Thin Places"

The devil can both tempt and provide. We often give in to temptation because we believe that forbidden fruit always tastes better. We are in a moment of history where we are about to leave the old world behind, yet we are still trying to hold onto what has already passed and make sense of its intricacies in order to fit our purpose.

The philosophy of Teleology argues that something has a reason or explanation because of its end purpose or goal. Aristotle proposed that there is a natural Teleology to the world and all things, claiming that an acorn's purpose is to become a fully grown oak tree, which is an intrinsic natural 'telos' or end of its purpose.

In recent centuries, many philosophers have argued against this type of philosophy. Madame Blavatsky and the introduction of Theology in her occult works have further complicated matters. Theology is the study of Gods and religion, yet Teleological discussions have been found in the study of Theology.

The classic Teleological argument for the existence of God suggests that a creator must exist because everything has been meticulously designed and an intelligent creator would have been necessary for the current state of things. This argument is based on the study of Theology, which includes Teleological discussions.

Norah's search for answers and her fascination with the thin place of Iona, where the veil between the elemental kingdom and our world is believed to be closer, became an irresistible calling for her. She was driven by a deep desire to uncover things that had not yet been written into existence and to be close to the faerie realm. Norah had been ready for this journey for a long time, carrying the scars of grief with her. Ultimately, Iona became her purpose and her end.

By 1929, Norah had developed a friendship with her housekeeper, referred to in newspapers at the time as Mrs. Varney. Little is known about her or her husband, and the ancestry records available are basic at best. In the book "Scotland's Unsolved Mysteries" by Richard Wilson, published in 1989, the author states that:

"Miss Farnario [sic], accompanied by a lady friend who would soon leave her to her own fateful devices, made her pilgrimage from London in August 1928."

Death on Iona

The high cross through the arched front of Iona Abbey by Mick Haupt.

It is one of the only references of Norah having travelled to the island with another person. And as you can see, the spelling of Fornario in this instance becomes Farnario, I would suspect through misinterpretation of available records or from another source. But the friend aspect is curious because it stands to reason that Norah would have travelled to Iona with someone else to help her, due to the vast amount of luggage she took with her.

"She intended to stay on the island for an indefinite period to seek the peace and serenity that had eluded her in London. She would use the quiet to write about, and pursue her study of, telepathy, faith-healing, and other mystic subjects. She stayed for the first few nights in the home of a Mrs. Macdonald. When her lady friend left to go back to London, she moved from the lodgings to Cameron Croft."

Wilson clearly did his research, and the mention of Cameron Croft is one that we'll explore further in the next section. It is also the only mention on record of Norah having stayed with the MacDonald's before moving in with the Camerons. And no mention of the MacRaes which plague internet posts and forums.

We know that Norah lived a relatively reclusive life, aside from building acquaintances in the occult world, she wasn't known to have held her own gatherings or conversed with many friends. But someone with such wealth and interest in secret societies may have had friends in higher places whom she conversed with on many occasions.

Though it is clear that the likes of Dion Fortune ended their friendship for reasons previously discussed. My

Death on Iona

assumption is that the lady friend mentioned in the news reports and in Wilson's book, was most likely Mrs. Varney.

As a housekeeper, Mrs. Varney would have been privy to a lot of information regarding Norah's private life, and as a servant, would have been requested to travel with her to Iona. It seems unlikely that one of Norah's peers would have travelled with her to Iona, help settle her, then leave a few days later. More unlikely that one of her peers would have helped drag the large amount of luggage she took with her.

Mrs. Varney, her housekeeper at Kew, said yesterday that Miss Fonario [sic] did not believe in doctors, and was 'always curing people by telepathy.' If people would not let her heal them she would moan and cry piteously, but she was otherwise cheerful and happy. A letter she sent to Mrs. Varney last week stated – 'Do not be surprised if you do not hear from me for a long time. I have a terrible healing case.'

Glasgow Herald, 27th November 1929.

The above was taken from the Glasgow Herald, eight days after Norah's body was found. Norah was sending letters to Mrs. Varney to keep in contact and most likely inform her of when she might be returning. The last letter was an omen in itself, that mentioned the terrible case of healing, and has since been lost to the corridors of time. Upon the news of Norah's death, no other came forward to disclose they had received letters, and I suspect that not many people would have known she was on Iona.

The journey to Iona from London in 1929 would not have been quick, and in fact, it's not the quickest route today. In a direct line from Central London to Iona, the distance is 420 miles (675km). Which, if there was a direct road or train track would take approximately six hours on a good day. But there is no direct route, and if there is no car then it's a bit trickier. There is no evidence to suggest Norah owned a vehicle and it was unlikely that a servant like Mrs. Varney would have done in the 1920s.

To travel from London to Iona without a car, it's much the same today as it was in 1929. Take a train from London to Glasgow then another train from Glasgow to Oban, board the ferry from Oban to Craignure on the Isle of Mull, travel across Mull to Fionnphort then board another ferry to Iona.

In the 1920s there was one daily bus on Mull which took passengers across the island from Craignure to Fionnphort. All in all, and even today, it's a long journey, and in 1929 would have been far more challenging.

It seems likely that Norah would have planned to stay with the Camerons before arriving, as to take so much luggage to a relatively remote island would have been fruitless if accommodation had not been sorted beforehand.

Death on Iona

That luggage included many personal items such as her typewriter, a chair, a case full of paper and ink, and many personal items of clothing and occult paraphernalia. She wasn't planning to stay on Iona for just a few days and saw it as a retreat of sorts, to escape the madness of London and write in peace.

In late August or early September, after the bulk of the tourist season had died down, Norah arrived on Iona. Just over two months later, her nude body was found exposed to the elements, dead of an apparent occult ritual.

Death on Iona

The Loneliness of Time

There have been numerous accounts of where Norah stayed while on Iona, with many mistakenly attributing her lodging to Mrs. Macrae. However, during my research, I was fortunate enough to connect with Iona historian Mairi MacArthur, who provided a wealth of knowledge and helped clarify some facts. It is worth noting that Ms. MacArthur is also related to one of the individuals who discovered Norah's body in 1929.

I had once made the mistake of taking online articles as fact, especially if so many said the same thing, and for many years believed that Norah had stayed with the mysterious Mrs. Macrae. The truth was hidden in plain sight, for a quick search of the island's records show that there was no Macrae family living on Iona in the 1920s.

Records and first-hand accounts indicate that Norah stayed with the Camerons and not a Mrs. Macrae, as many retellings of the tale tend to state. Calum Cameron, who was the Camerons 12-year-old son at the time, gave a first-hand account of Norah's stay in 1929. Calum was born in 1916 to his parents, Catherine

MacArthur and Donald Cameron, and raised on the family Croft. Donald was listed on the 1911 census in the Isle of Mull parish of Kilfinichen and Kilvickeon, which included Iona.

Calum had two older sisters, Catherine 'Katy' Ada Cameron and Mary Cameron, neither of whom has spoken about Norah's stay. The Camerons took in lodgers from time to time, mostly long-stays, but sometimes opened up rooms for the tourist season.

In 1911, James Morrison and Lily Mackay, both born in Glasgow and in their early teens, were listed as boarders at the Camerons' residence. The term "boarder" implied that they had a transient status or were long-term guests, but it is almost certain that James and Lily were placed there by the Parish Board as part of a social scheme implemented throughout the Highlands.

Children in cities, particularly Glasgow, who were orphaned or whose guardians were unfit to care for them, were placed with families in rural areas. The host families received financial assistance towards the children's upkeep.

When Norah arrived at the Camerons' house, Catherine was 50, Donald 66, Katy 21, and Mary 18, though Katy may have been on the mainland for education or work. The Camerons took in lodgers from time to time, mostly for long-stays, but sometimes opened up rooms for the tourist season.

Before the days of travel agents and online bookings, Norah would have written a letter or sent a telegram to the Camerons asking if there were any lodgings available, and with the amount of money she had, she would have offered a decent amount to keep the Camerons happy after the peak season. It would have been a fruitless exercise to turn up on Iona with half her belongings without securing a place to stay.

Despite contemporary reports that Norah was frowned upon by the islanders for having such vastly different beliefs and dress sense, she was welcomed and respected, and she, in turn, respected the islanders. There was a mutual understanding that Norah was there on a retreat, and despite her different looks and mannerisms, she was well-liked. Norah was recorded as wearing flowing dresses with fancy adornments, wild hair, and wilder accessories.

She stayed in the attic of the Camerons' house and set up her typewriter on a small table along with her writing chair. She spent most of her time writing and exploring the island, usually walking along the shorelines.

However, one must be cautious when relying on oral historical accounts, as much can be embellished or misremembered. The same applies to written accounts, particularly those in newspapers. Norah believed that she had lived on the island in a previous incarnation, although it was not recorded how she viewed that incarnation. It could have been as a faerie from another realm or a religious human incarnation.

There is no mention of who she was in her past life, nor is it recorded anywhere. Nonetheless, it is likely that she believed she was a former resident of the island, regardless of that person's religion or views. She simply lived on the island, as one with the island itself.

Iona Abbey and Nunnery by Caroline Hall.

Another reason for heading to Iona to write was quite simply – quietness. For London in the early 20th Century was loud, probably louder than it is today. The end of the First World War brought with it an industrial and economic age the likes of which had never been seen before. For Norah, someone who wanted to be at one with nature and the other realms, London was restrictive and busy, while Iona was free and quiet.

Writing retreats are still popular today, and as I write this, I wonder how calming the view of ancient shorelines would be on the imaginative faculty rather than the bustle of Camden that flows over me at this moment.

Calum Cameron, in his discussion with Richard Wilson, said that Norah had come to Iona to pursue her study of telepathy, healing, and other mystic subjects that Calum didn't quite understand at the time, nor chose to understand after the fact. 58 years after Norah had stayed in his family's home, Calum remembered parts of her stay that intrigue to this day.

> *"She took lonely walks at night to study the island, sometimes to the large ground mound of Fairy Hill, said to harbour the spirits of the pre-Christian dead. She kept her curtains closed because she believed she could see the faces of her previous 'patients' in the clouds. She kept two oil lamps that she kept burning in her room. She behaved as if she were being hunted."*

Calum Cameron, 1989.

While the Fairy Hill was mostly common knowledge, the fact that Norah felt she was being hunted is curious, not least because embellishments have been made to suggest that she was being physically or mentally hunted.

The notion of being mentally hunted is similar to the psychic attacks written about by Dion Fortune, who believed that Norah had died from being psychically attacked. Some researchers have gone so far as to assume that she was killed by a mystery person or thing on the island that was physically hunting her.

However, Calum Cameron states that she only acted as if she was being hunted. Acting out of fear is very different from experiencing it as reality, and there is no evidence to suggest that someone was physically hunting her. It is possible that someone on the island may have followed her out of curiosity, but for no other reason.

That she was acting paranoid and worried may indicate that she was in the midst of a mental health crisis and suffering from delusions, which can seem as real as the book you are holding to someone who is experiencing it.

Delusions can result from mental illness, but they can also stem from general beliefs, such as thinking that aliens are hiding behind clouds or that a neighbour is a serial killer. However, delusions that arise from mental illness are often classified as psychotic disorders, previously known as paranoid disorders or paranoid delusions, and can be detrimental to the individual experiencing them.

Though it's important to note that delusions are not always as strange as they are often portrayed, and individuals can usually function relatively normally in society while still incorporating their delusion into their daily life. Psychotic breaks, which include delusions as a symptom, can also be indicative of another mental health disorder.

While schizophrenia can include delusions as a symptom, delusions themselves are not a direct cause of the disorder. Instead, delusions can be a negative consequence of various mental disorders, similar to self-harm. Traumatic experiences such as grief or abuse, as well as a genetic predisposition, may contribute to the development of delusional disorders.

In Norah's case, her involvement in the occult and her search for solace in the thin place could also have played a role in her mental state leading up to her death. Regardless of the cause, delusions are just as real to the individual experiencing them as reality is to anyone else, and it is crucial that they receive the necessary support and treatment to manage their symptoms.

It is likely that Norah was suffering from delusions based on her beliefs, but it is important to first examine the circumstances of her death and the embellishments that have grown around her story.

Death on Iona

The Realm of the Dead

Norah would occasionally spend days alone in the attic room, focusing on writing, typing, or meditating. She seemed to be very focused on something beyond her general health. In the days leading up to her death, she would often take long walks along the shoreline or over the hills of the island, lost in thought as she searched for a reason for her visit to Iona. Some days, she would sit on the shore and stare out at the islands beyond.

On the morning of Sunday, November 17th, Norah rushed down the stairs in a state of panic and told the Camerons that she had to leave the island immediately. She seemed to be in a state of great anxiety, as if someone was pursuing her and she had to escape. She mentioned that there was a ship without a rudder passing through the sky, carrying a message from the great beyond.

Before the Camerons could speak to her more, she had already dragged her luggage to the ferry port and sat on her bags, waiting for the ferry to come and take her away. An hour passed before it dawned on her that there were no ferries on Sundays, the Sabbath day, in

1929. Her anxiety and panic were replaced with defeat and dissatisfaction as she dragged her bags back to the house and retook residence in the attic.

Even though the Camerons knew that there were no ferries, they may have secretly hoped that Norah had found a way off the island and they could rent out the room again. When she came down for dinner that night, her panic had subsided, and she seemed calm and relaxed as usual.

"Aye, she was a'right on the Sunday night."

Calum Cameron.

Before we jump into the theories surrounding her death, let's look again at the mental health aspect of her case. It's not uncommon for those who are suffering from a mental illness to accept their delusions, which can change their demeanour.

That Norah was intent on escaping the island, only to return and make peace with herself, is akin to an 'endgame' in mental health. It is where someone comes to accept that a path has been chosen for them regardless of how they want it to play out.

After dinner, she retreated to her room, rejuvenated and somewhat relaxed, much to the Camerons delight. But later that Sunday night, Norah walked out of the croft and never returned. The following morning, Mary Cameron took a substantial breakfast to her room, as she did most days.

"Calum's sister took breakfast to her room and knocked. No answer but could smell burning. She entered to see the fireplace lit, oil lamps near the typewriter lit, and no sign of Norah. The Camerons immediately searched the shoreline and whistled."

Richard Wilson.

At some point during the night, Norah had walked off into the darkness. She had a habit of going on long walks and the Monday morning mist was mostly an attraction to her. Thinking she had gone on a long walk, the Camerons let her be. Until the late afternoon, when the dusk had started to set in and the cold breeze picked up.

Realising it was getting cold, the Camerons walked along a small part of the shoreline, whistling and calling out to her. Judging by the clothes left in Norah's room, it was their belief that she had gone out unprepared for the weather conditions and they were justifiably concerned. When there was no sign of Norah on the Monday afternoon, and when she didn't return for dinner, the Camerons raised the alarm.

A search team was organised, and many islanders searched until the early evening, and some continued into the night, to find the missing woman. It was agreed to continue the search on Tuesday morning, although there were already suspicions that Norah may

Death on Iona

have met her fate on the shoreline, where the waves could be dangerous. The seas around Scotland, especially around smaller islands like Iona, tend to be rough.

By Tuesday morning, most of the island had been searched, and the theory of Norah having drowned was becoming more likely. In contrast to later accounts, the Fairy Hill was searched and not overlooked by the islanders.

Many accounts place Norah's body on Sìthean Mòr, the Fairy Hill, which would make sense as she was there to connect with the "thin place" and what better place than where Columba conversed with angels? Sìthean Mòr is next to one of the main roads on the island, and people were walking past it all the while the search was going on.

The truth of the discovery is far less poetic but eternally tragic. On early Tuesday afternoon, two farmers, Hector Maclean and Hector MacNiven, left the search to carry out livestock duties.

They found Norah's naked body a mile away from the Camerons' house. It's important to point out that the landscape of Iona is not simply flat, as many have written. The highest point of Iona is Dùn Ì, which is 101 m (331 ft) above sea level. Even with the residents searching the entire island, there are hills that are not easy to search, and it would be easy to miss a body among them.

One of the main suspicions of the mystery is that two days had passed before her body was found, and for such a small island, it seemed strange that she wasn't found before. But if you were to walk the hills of Iona, close to the location where Norah was found, it would become obvious how difficult the search would have been. The moorland south of the loch is rough, heathery ground full of hummocks and hollows.

Nowadays, mountain rescue or the coastguard use drones to search the sometimes harsh landscape of the Scottish Highlands. Had Norah gone missing on Iona today, it's likely that her body would have been found quickly. Back in 1929, the islanders had nothing more than their own knowledge of the island and some farm dogs.

It seems logical that Norah's body was not discovered earlier due to weather conditions, the landscape, and the fact that a proper search was not undertaken until one day into her disappearance.

Some occult researchers have suggested that the two-day gap between Norah's disappearance and being found was due to her succeeding in her goals. It has been written that Norah managed to pass through the thin place to the Elemental Kingdom, where she conversed with the faeries before returning to Iona and dying of exposure. However, throughout recorded history, there is no written evidence of someone physically passing through a thin place. Most experiences are spiritual or psychological in nature.

Death on Iona

When Norah was found, she was naked and lying on her side with her face turned up to the sky. There was no decomposition as her body had frozen in the bitter November frost. The two Hector's raised the alarm, and across the island, there came a realisation that there was to be no happy ending to the search for the New Age woman from London.

A coroner from Mull was called in, who concluded rather quickly that Norah had died from exposure the evening before, on the 18th, and listed 'exposure to the elements' as the cause of death. He also noted some scratches on her feet but no other marks. These marks would later be used as 'proof' that Norah was murdered.

Officials from Mull searched the attic room at the Camerons and found an address for Norah's uncle and aunt, who were based in London. They contacted the family, who replied that they or Norah's father were unable to travel to Iona to collect the body. In their place, a London-based solicitor was sent to make the final arrangements. Even though Norah died in Scotland, her will and administration were administered in England at the behest of her father. Her will was published in the papers:

Marie Edith Emily Nora Fornario of 73 Mortlake Road Richmond Surrey, spinster, died 18 November 1929 at the Island of Iona Inner Hebrides. N.B. Administration (limited) London 24 May 1930 to Barclays Bank Limited attorney of Guiseppe Fornario. Effects £424 18s 6d. Index of Wills and Administrations 1858-1966. (FF12754).

It is unclear if the house on Mortlake Road in Richmond was sold off for legal fees or passed on to Norah's uncle and auntie. Today, the tree-lined street boasts large detached and semi-detached properties worth a lot of money. If the house had been inherited by her family, they likely would have sold it since they had no need for it. What happened to Mrs. Varney, the housekeeper, has never been recorded.

Despite the mystery surrounding her death, the people of Iona showed kindness by rallying together to raise enough money to bury Norah on the island. Practically every soul on the island attended her impressive funeral on Friday 22nd November, and Norah was buried in the graveyard of kings at St. Odhrain's chapel in the grounds of Iona Abbey. Her modest gravestone bears her initials and date of death, 18th November 1929.

The story of Norah's mysterious death quickly spread through the newspapers, as reporters focused on the occult aspect of the case. As a result, the story was embellished across the world.

Death on Iona

The Persistence of Myth

"A young woman dies from exposure on the Scottish island of Iona."

That is what the headlines should have read in a logical world. However, there was mystery at the heart of Norah's death, not least due to her affiliations with the occult, which had only recently gone mainstream in the early 20th century, but also due to the circumstances of her death. The discussions that follow are based less on conspiracy theory and more on theoretical assumptions based on logic and probability.

I believe it is entirely probable that Norah suffered a psychotic break and succumbed to the elements one night while searching for a portal to the thin place. Under the same theoretical assumptions, it is possible to conclude that Norah was killed via psychic attack, murdered by islanders, abducted by aliens, killed by beings from beyond the thin place, or murdered by a fellow occultist under cover of darkness.

Though all of these assumptions beyond a mental breakdown are outlandish, they are not without basis. As Norah's story was retold in the century that followed, those assumptions became fact, and those facts became historical inaccuracies. We can begin with the newspapers of the time, which, in their desire to sell more copies, embellished facts from various sources.

During my research, I contacted the Oban Times regarding clippings from November 1929 and was told the following.

> *We do not have a digital archive and our bound copies are in storage at another location, so are not readily accessible. I would recommend that you contact the National Library of Scotland in Edinburgh or the Mitchell Library in Glasgow, which both have our papers on microfiche.*

Though both the National Library and Mitchell Library have some copies of the Oban Times on record, they are few and far between. The offline storage of the Oban Times has since been unconfirmed, meaning they may or may not exist.

It would certainly have helped in the research, as the Oban Times was the local paper of the day, and there was mention in other newspapers about an Oban

Death on Iona

Times story titled 'Fate of an Iona Visitor - London Woman Found Dead.'

However, the Oban Times story was proven a moot point as it was dated the 30th of November 1929, eleven days after Norah's body was found. The earliest press cutting was five days before that.

THE IONA TRAGEDY.

Woman of Italian Parentage Who Hated Italy. Latest details received by the Press and Journal concerning Miss F, whose body was found on Iona on Tuesday last, suggest strongly that she was an unusual type.

Page four of the Aberdeen Press and Journal on Monday 25th November.

Variations of the same small press release were found in the Wednesday 27th November editions of the Birmingham Daily Gazette, Hartlepool Northern Daily Mail, Sheffield Independent, Western Daily Press, Leeds Mercury, The Scotsman, Gloucestershire Echo, Londonderry Sentinel, and the Hull Daily Mail. On the same day, 27th, the Glasgow Herald ran a more detailed piece.

Once, she announced her intention to fast for 40 days but was persuaded to give it up after a fortnight. She dressed in a long cape-like garment made by herself, and never wore a hat. A letter she sent to Mrs. Varney last week stated – "Do not be surprised if you do not hear from me for a long time. I have a terrible healing case."

Glasgow Herald, 27th November 1929.

The story of the terrible healing case that Norah wrote about in her letter to her housekeeper is often included in retellings of the story. Norah was known to go into trances and remain in them for several hours at a time, and sometimes even longer.

It is not clear from the letter whether the terrible case of healing was for herself or someone else, but it would be logical to assume that she was trying to heal her own mind rather than that of another. The report then goes on to include some unusual additions that other sources did not have.

It is stated that Miss Fonario's [sic] unclothed body was lying on a large cross which had been cut out of the turf, apparently with a knife which was lying nearby. Round the neck was a silver chain and cross. Among weird stories now in circulation in the Western Islands regarding Miss Fonario are mysterious remarks about blue lights having been seen near the body and of a cloaked man.

A number of letters, said to be of a strange character, have been taken possession of by the police, who have passed them on to the Procurator-Fiscal for his consideration. Miss Fonario had been heard again and again to express hatred of Italy and Italians, and her hostility to them was carried so far that she refused to meet them.

Glasgow Herald, 27th November 1929.

Now we need to examine exactly what they were talking about and how they arrived at some of the more outlandish conclusions. One of the mysteries of the case is the occult ritualistic nature of her death, as many stories claim she was found on a cross with a dagger in one hand and letters of unusual characters in the other.

In the years that followed, a conclusion was drawn that Norah had travelled to Iona to perform an occult ritual to reach the other side, using one of the world's "thin places," and that, in some way, she had succeeded. It's easy to see why this story has persisted: an unusual-looking woman, with occult links, dies in strange circumstances.

The Glasgow Herald mentions blue lights near the body and a cloaked man. The blue lights could have been reported by either a local or someone who had heard of the story on the mainland and mentioned them as an afterthought. Writers in the years that followed took this to be evidence of fairies around Norah's body or in the sky above her.

However, if blue lights were seen near the body, someone must have known the body was there. It would have been unusual not to investigate when an island-wide search was underway. It's also possible that the event of Norah's death had affected some of the islanders, and when blue lights were seen near the location where she died, someone may have thought they were unusual.

The blue lights seen near Norah's body at the time of her death have been subject to various interpretations over the years, ranging from fairies to extra-terrestrial activity. However, it is more likely that the lights were either a reflection from a passing ship or part of the search effort being conducted by the authorities.

It is also possible that they were caused by natural phenomena such as the Northern Lights, which are known to occur in that part of Scotland. Reports of blue lights in the sky are not uncommon and are often attributed to electrical wires, buildings, or satellites. In 2021 alone, there were sightings of blue lights in various parts of the world, including the UK and Mexico.

While some may be tempted to interpret such sightings as evidence of supernatural activity, a more rational explanation is usually available. Ultimately, the exact cause of the blue lights seen near Norah's body may never be known. However, it is important to approach such phenomena with a healthy dose of scepticism and rational thinking, rather than jumping to supernatural conclusions.

The Glasgow Herald story was published eleven days after Norah was found. From my research in the field of true crime, people tend to remember things slightly differently than what they witnessed when talking to the press about an incident.

The stories of the cloaked figure could have been Norah herself, as she was known to wear one of her homemade cloaks. However, one wild theory suggests that Aleister Crowley travelled to Iona in secret to murder Norah because she was close to discovering a life-changing occult secret. It is suggested that Crowley used a small boat to get to the island, lured Norah from her attic room, and led her to a barren part of the island to perform an occult ritual that killed her.

Firstly, it's important to state that anyone involved in the occult is no more likely to commit murder than people with any number of other hobbies, religious beliefs, or cultural tastes. It is one of the great misconceptions that occultism is inherently evil when it is not. Crowley never murdered anyone in his life, and though his beliefs were considered "dark," he had no reason to be connected to Norah in any way.

It is possible that they briefly met due to their involvement in the same groups, but it is unlikely that their meeting was anything more than a passing of souls. Could the person in the cloak have been a murderer, meaning that Norah was murdered by another human?

It is unlikely that someone came from the mainland to kill Norah or murder her at all, as we'll see in later chapters. But what about the cross on the ground beneath her and the knife? Calum Cameron recalls the discovery of the body.

> *"It was just an ordinary kitchen knife which could have done no harm to anybody. She just died of exposure as the doctor said, it's that*

simple. There was no cross, she was just digging in the ground, maybe trying to get to the fairies inside. She was a disturbed woman, that's all."

Calum Cameron.

Oral historical records are not always reliable, but it seemed Calum was pretty adamant in believing in grounded reality rather than extraordinary occurrences, as his whole family would have been. I've spoken to people who live on Iona and Mull, and though some feel a spiritual affinity with the islands, none had ever felt fear that they would be murdered or that such a crime would visit their shores.

Yet, one such murder did take place in 2018 on the nearby Isle of Bute when six-year-old Alesha MacPhail was abducted and murdered by 16-year-old Aaron Campbell. He was caught quickly and ultimately sentenced to 27 years, but it remains proof that murder does and has visited the islands around Scotland.

Could it have happened in November 1929? It is absolutely possible that Norah was murdered, but due to the very nature of her character and history, it remains unlikely, improbable, and, as we'll read later, illogical.

It's clear the islanders believed wholeheartedly that Norah was suffering from mental issues and that her death was a tragic accident caused by exposure to the frost. In any instance, many of the islanders were the last people to have seen Norah alive, and their testimonies as eye-witnesses to her condition could be the closest we get to the truth of the matter. But as we've seen, less than one week later, facts were already being embellished in newspapers across the country and soon, the world.

In the Northern Whig on 27th November, an Irish newspaper of the time, and under the heading of 'Strange Iona Story', they detailed the fact that Norah had travelled to the great beyond and back again many times.

A strange story of the death of a strange woman reached London yesterday from Iona, the famous island off the West Coast of Scotland. The woman, Miss Nora Emily Fonario, of Mortlake Road, Kew, London, was found dead on a lonely hillside at midnight on Tuesday of last week. Her unclothed body was lying on a large cross which had been cut out of the turf, apparently with a knife which was lying nearby. Round the neck was a silver chain and cross.

Several times she said she had been to the far beyond and had come back to life after spending some time in another world. A number of letters, said to be of strange character, have been taken possession of by the police, who have passed them on to the Procurator Fiscal for his consideration.

Northern Whig, 27th November 1929.

The report mentions that Norah had travelled to the far beyond, which is a euphemism for going into trances or connecting with the astral and psychic planes. They also mention, like other reports, that a silver chain and cross were found around her neck, which she always wore.

Some reports claim that the silver had blackened overnight. However, if the cross was solid silver, then it tends to darken over time, especially when exposed to sweat on skin. A silver item of jewellery turning black is not a cause for much concern beyond simple rules of chemistry.

The report also mentions that letters were taken by the police and handed to the Procurator Fiscal, who prosecutes all criminal cases in Scotland. While one might think that the Procurator Fiscal's involvement indicates that a crime had been committed, they also have a responsibility to investigate all sudden, suspicious, and unexplained deaths in Scotland, which is why the police handed over some of Norah's belongings to the Procurator Fiscal office.

I contacted Police Scotland, the local Procurator Fiscal offices, and Glasgow Life, which is a repository of information that includes police files, to find out what records they had on file and where the letters were, if they existed.

"Police Scotland does not hold any of the information requested. In terms of Section 17 of the Act (FOIA), this letter represents a formal notice that information is not held."

I followed up with various official offices, local archives, and historical databases across Scotland, but sadly, much of the information that once existed has been lost over time.

"National Records of Scotland does not have any information relating to Ms Fornario. NRS archivists conducted a comprehensive search of our catalogue and found no reference to the case there. They have also been unable to trace any reference to letters of Ms Fornario being held in our archives."

So what were these letters spoken about in the press of the time? Some say that she was found clutching onto a handful of letters, and it was these letters that were taken away by the coroner to hand to the police. The two Hectors who found Norah made no observation of any letters or papers near her body.

It's more likely that the letters of unusual character were removed from the attic room. The fact that they seemed unusual to the police probably meant they contained various symbols relating to any one of the occult groups that Norah belonged to or was attempting to create.

The story of the strange death on Iona reached the United States and was written about in various newspapers from Florida to California. The Border Cities Star, the paper of Windsor, Ontario, ran the story on their front page under the heading of *Isle of*

Death on Iona

Ionia Has Baffling Mystery. It too was dated 27th November 1929, which meant that word had travelled fast.

Police of Argyllshire trudged the windy hills of this sacred island today seeking the cause of the death of Miss Norah Emily Fornario, who believed in fairies. The 32-year-old-woman, who was said to be a psychic was found lying dead on a bleak hillside, her clothes torn off and her body lying on a cross which had been roughly dug in the ground with a knife found nearby. She apparently died of exposure.

Around her life, the natives had built a legend of the supernatural. Her strange end on the island which has long been a mecca of pilgrims because it is said to be the burial ground of 60 kings of Scotland, Norway, France, and Ireland, added to the superstition. The Western Highlanders said that the ghosts of monks slain by Norse raiders haunted the Island of Iona.

They talked, with some reticence, of how Miss Fornario claimed to be able to heal illness by telepathic powers. Her favourite spot was at St. Columba's Bay where St. Columba landed from Ireland in the year 563 and erected a monastery. The island is but three and one-half miles long, its soil strewn with the bones of pilgrims. The population is 500.

The Border Cities Star, 27th November 1929.

It's probably the most dramatic and poetic recapping of the event. The very fact the paper reports the island as Ionia and the residents as natives, suggests they were not too consumed with the facts of the death.

Telepathic powers, clothes torn off, body on a cross, burial ground of kings, ghosts of slain monks, Norse raiders, bones of pilgrims – it's no wonder the story captured the imaginations of those who read it, and who would go on to form their own opinions based on their own beliefs.

On 10th June 1930, the London Gazette printed the will and testimony of Norah.

Marie Edith Emily Nora Fornario, deceased. Pursuant to Trustee Act, 1925. NOTICE is hereby given that all persons having any debts, claims or demands against the estate of Marie Edith Emily Nora Fornario, of 73, Mortlake-road, Richmond, in the county of Surrey, who died on the eighteenth day of November, one thousand nine hundred and twenty-nine, at The Island of Iona, Inner Hebrides, in 'Scotland, intestate, and to whose estate letters of administration -were granted by the Principal Probate Registry of His Majesty's High Court of Justice on the twenty-fourth day of May, one thousand nine hundred and thirty, to Barclays Bank Limited, the lawful attorney of Guiseppe Fornario, the lawful Father of the deceased, are hereby required to send written particulars thereof to the Trustee Department, Barclays Bank Limited, 37, King William-street, London, E.G. 4, or to the undersigned, on or before the sixteenth day of August, one thousand nine hundred and thirty, after which date the said estate will be distributed, having regard only to the claims then notified.—Dated 6th June, 1930. DURRANT COOPER and HAMBLING, 70-71, Gracechurch-street, London, E.C. 3, (149) Solicitors to the Attorney.

I tracked down the solicitor mentioned in the Gazette who was sent to Iona to make the final arrangements, hoping he might have archived some of Norah's letters or belongings. The current iteration of the company is Lovell, White & King, which merged with the Durrant Piesse law firm to create Lovell White Durrant.

Durrant Piesse itself was formed by the 1973 merger of two long-established City firms, Durrant Cooper & Hambling, founded in 1893. In short, the law firm had changed so many times that any records from the 1920s have long been destroyed.

When I asked if their predecessors had passed on any of Norah's belongings to family members or sent them to her London address, they had no way of ascertaining it. They suggested that if there was anything of value, it would have appeared in the will, and it didn't. Most other belongings would have been destroyed or sold to settle fees.

A living descendant of Norah's family may have kept some of her letters, but almost 100 years later, and after speaking to many people, it seems certain that her writings and letters have been lost and confined to the corridors of time. The most frustrating aspect of this case and Norah's death is that her letters and belongings have either been destroyed or misplaced.

Perhaps her writings held the key to her death and could shed some light on her thoughts at the time. As Calum Cameron said, she would type and write a voluminous amount of work. Based on her minimal

Death on Iona

available writings, we can only imagine how insightful and valuable they may have been.

On 29th May 2001, Scotland on Sunday from The Scotsman ran a story about private detective Dr. Ron Halliday and a psychic friend who headed to Iona to solve the mystery of Norah Fornario, under the headline 'Hoping to solve Iona's mystery'.

She sought refuge on the island known as Scotland's spiritual haven in an attempt to escape the unknown evil forces she claimed were trying to kill her. At night she would go into a trance to contact the spirits roaming the island. But just when she felt ready to leave the spiritual protection of Iona's Christians, tragedy struck.

With her bags packed and the farmhouse where she had been staying tidied, Miss Fornario thought she would take one last wander around the surroundings of her temporary home. She was never seen alive again. The alarm was raised when the 33-year-old did not return to the croft. Her naked body was found that afternoon lying on the Fairy Mound to the south of Loch Staonaig, an area associated with black magic.

Miss Fornario's body had been laid out on a religious cloak. There was a silver chain around her neck and a long knife in her hand. A crude cross had been cut out of the turf beneath her body. However, despite the strange circumstances surrounding her death, police reports ruled out foul play and her death certificate records "exposure to the elements and heart failure" as the cause of death.

The Scotsman, 29th May 2001.

Before we investigate what else was in this report, it's important to point out that there are so many inaccuracies with The Scotsman's report, 72 years after Norah's death, that it's difficult to know where to begin. The story highlights how even modern-day newspapers embellish aspects of her death, which seem preferable to the facts and eye-witness statements of the time.

Norah sought refuge on the island as a retreat and for spiritual exploration, not to escape unknown evil forces that she claimed were trying to kill her. In all my research, Norah never wrote or told anyone that someone was trying to kill her.

Her body was not found on the Fairy Mound; it was found one mile away from the Camerons' house in the South Hills. The two Hectors found her naked on the hills and not resting on a religious cloak. The robe she was wearing was a normal one found many meters from her death site, which suggests that it had blown away at some point before or after she died.

There are no eye-witness reports citing a cloak, let alone a religious one. There was no knife in her hands, the knife was found a few metres from the body, and was deemed by Calum Cameron to be a kitchen knife that she had possibly used at some point to hack the ground beneath her.

There is the assumption she was trying to hack her way through to the fairy realm. Maybe, as the cold and delirium set in, she thought she was on the Fairy Hill, and cutting her way through was going to work. It's also possible she got so confused, couldn't find shelter and tried to dig a hole to wait in until morning – though unlikely, as the weather wasn't too adverse that night.

The report goes on to state the death is to be reinvestigated by Ron Halliday and his unnamed but 'qualified' psychic friend, as they both believe she had been killed by black magic. They hoped to find new clues as to the cause of Norah's death. Ron wholeheartedly believed she had been murdered.

> *"She went to Iona to protect herself from something but she ended up dying in strange circumstances. Accidental death was recorded but that cannot be the case. The way her body was found suggests otherwise. Now we are out to show once and for all that some other factor or power could have been responsible. Despite what was recorded at the time, we believe the police just brushed it all under the carpet."*

Dr. Ron Halliday.

The local police were contacted for the report, but they said, as I later found out, that there were no records available for that time, nor was there any record relating to Norah. However, they did say that the circumstances of her death would have been fully investigated at the time.

Regarding Halliday, in his 2001 book Scotland's X-Files, he briefly mentioned Norah's story. It is unclear whether it was a coincidence or a deliberate marketing strategy that the book was released around the same time as The Scotsman's story.

Found in the hills of Loch Staonaig. She was naked except for the robe of the Order of Alpha and Omega. The soles of her feet were bloody.

Scotland's X-Files

There has been no addendum to the original piece or no new information in the past 20 years. Incidentally, Ron Halliday never returned to Iona, and no new investigation took place. According to the two Hectors, Norah was not found in a robe from the Order of the Alpha et Omega, nor did the cloak found nearby have any occult symbols on.

Modern lack of faith in police, governments, and authority, has seen a rising number of writers and researchers who believe Norah's death was no accident, and as such believe she was murdered.

Death on Iona

The Timeless Tale

After the news reports and subsequent retellings in the Occult Journal, as well as Dion Fortune's own work, the next major piece regarding the mysterious death on Iona was a poem by Helen Cruickshank, titled *Ballad of the Lost Ladye*. It was published in 1947 as part of the Iona Anthology by Florence Marian McNeill and is now in the public domain.

O siller, siller shone the mune

An' quaiet swang the door,

An' eerie skraighed the flaughtered gulls

As she gaed by the shore.

O saft tae her the meadow girse,

But set wi' rock the hill,

An' scored wi' bluid her ladye feet

Or she cam' the place intill.

Death on Iona

The sheen o' steel was in her hand,
The sheen o' stars in her een,
An' she wad open the fairy hill
An' she wad let oot the queen.

There cam' a shepherd owre the hill
When day began tae daw;
And is this noo a seggit ewe
Or flourish frae the schaw?

It wasna lamb nor seggit ewe
Nor flourish frae the schaw,
It was the ladye bright an' still,
But she had won awa'.

The peace an' loveliness upon
Her broo said, 'Lat abee,
Here fand I that I sairly socht,
Ye needna peety mee.'

If you find the language difficult, the ballad-like poem is about the unexplained discovery of a woman's body early in the morning beside the Fairy Hill. Cruickshank may have taken creative liberty, or used old newspapers to claim that the lady, assumed to be Norah, was found on the Fairy Hill, when in fact she wasn't. Her creative interpretation may have contributed to the belief that Norah was found there.

The next retelling was by Alasdair Alpin MacGregor in his 1955 book "The Ghost Book: Strange Hauntings in Britain". In the section titled "Haunted Iona", Alasdair recounts the story as told to him by Lucy Bruce and the coincidentally named Iona Cammell. In his version of the events, Alasdair refers to Norah as Nessa, which is the first known instance of that name being used.

> *Of the mystical poetry she wrote, I have never seen anything. But I have heard from those competent to judge that it was of a very high order. Exactly what these were, nobody could quite say.*
>
> Alasdair Alpin MacGregor

If I could go back in time to those few days from Norah coming down to dinner to her being found dead, that's where and when I'd go, not least to discover what really happened but to read the voluminous work she had produced while on the island.

Death on Iona

When, however, she began to speak of visions that she had seen in the heavens, and of messages received from the spirit world, they (the Camerons) were quite horrified. To them, that faraway look they had seen in her eyes now denoted either madness or something diabolical. Yet, their native predisposition toward anything of a supernatural character tempered their attitude.

Mrs. Cameron chanced to notice that the jewellery Nessa was wearing had become black. Unable to restrain curiosity any longer, Mrs Cameron sought of her the explanation, only to be told that this was always happened to her jewellery when she wore it.

Not until the afternoon did Hector MacLean, of Sligneach, and Hector MacNiven, of Maol Farm, find her. She lay between the Machar and Loch Staonaig, in a hollow in the chilly moor. She was quite dead, and, except for a silver chain turned black, quite naked.

How, otherwise [than in a trance], could a woman, unable in the ordinary way to proceed on foot more than a few hundred yards at a time, have travelled so far over territory so precipitous, so broken, so perilous? She must have reached that hollow of death by hurrying through the heather and over the rocks on the tip of her toes.

The Ghost Book: Strange Hauntings In Britain (1955).

As far as I could tell, the book was never republished and is extremely difficult to get hold of, except for one copy in the British Library. There were many things that Alasdair had written that were true. He was correct about the two Hectors, who were only mentioned in one other book post-1955, and of course, this one. He also states that her body was found in the hollow of the chilly moor and doesn't lay claim to her being found on the Fairy Hill.

I wanted to find out more about the two women who recounted the tale of Norah to Alasdair. It is unusual that he hadn't gone to Iona to speak directly to the residents there. Though he lists Iona Cammell as a resident, she was not.

> *"Iona Cammell and her husband Charles were occasional visitors to Iona. Miss Lucy Bruce, who had an interest in spirituality, built a house on the island ca 1928 and holidayed there until her death, in Edinburgh, in 1962."*

Mairi MacArthur, Iona Historian.

It is unclear why Alasdair chose to take the testimony of two non-resident visitors to the island. The report of Norah's silver jewellery turning black has been used as evidence of her being psychically attacked or involved in occult practices. While silver does turn black over time, it is unlikely for it to turn black overnight.

Some researchers have suggested that the high acidity level in Norah's sweat may have caused the silver to blacken quickly, but this is unlikely and has been taken out of context. It is also strange how the two visitors were able to recall so many details of Norah's interactions with the Camerons unless they had direct contact with Mrs. Cameron.

Despite some inconsistencies, Alasdair's story, based on the testimony of Iona Cammell and Lucy Bruce, remains one of the more credible accounts of Norah's death.

The first mention of the name Norah outside of the co-masonic membership rolls and Mrs. MacRae was in Francis King's Modern Ritual Magic: The Rise of Western Occultism, originally published in England in 1970 and in the United States as The Rites of Modern Occult Magic in 1971. The book begins with a dramatic introduction.

"Dion Fortune actually accused Mrs. Mathers of the psychic murder of Miss Norah Fornario, a member of the Alpha et Omega, who had died in unusual and mysterious circumstances. In the autumn of 1929, when she was thirty-five years of age, she left her London home and travelled to the 'Holy Isle' of Iona."

Francis King

It is now known from historical records that Norah was 33 and not 35, a substantial difference of two years. Dion Fortune never accused Moina Mathers of psychic murder; she only taught people how to be prepared for possible psychic attacks. Moina Mathers had died eighteen months before Norah's death, so carrying out a psychic attack from beyond the grave would have been quite impossible.

She boarded with Mrs. MacRae, a native of the island, who fascinated her lodger with stories of mysterious happenings and the folklore of the Hebrides. Mrs. MacRae was equally fascinated by her guest whom she suspected of indulging in what she was later to call 'mystical practices'.

Her fascination turned to alarm, however, when Miss Fornario told her that she had recently undergone a trance lasting a full week and thought that there was a strong possibility that she might again undergo such a trance in the near future — under no circumstances, added Miss Fornario, was Mrs. MacRae to call a physician.

Ritual Magic, 1970.

King's book is the first to mention Mrs. MacRae, which we know to be incorrect. There were no MacRaes living on the island at the time Norah was there. She certainly didn't lodge with a MacRae; we know that now to be the Camerons. Furthermore, it is the first instance of the notion that Norah would go into a full trance and that one should not call the doctor during such a state.

This section has been repeated throughout history but has no written evidence before this to clarify it. Clearly, the name of the people involved was wrong. So it was with curiosity that King didn't place her body at the Fairy Hill, but there were further embellishments.

Except for the black cloak of the Hiereus (an important officer in a Golden Dawn Temple) the body was naked. Round its neck was a blackened silver chain, in its hand was a large steel knife, the soles of its feet were torn and had bled heavily although the heels were intact.

Clearly Miss Fornario had ran for a considerable distance before she had come to her stopping place and cut into the turf the large cross, on which, so the examining physician said, she had met her death by heart failure. I think it certain that either Miss Fornario was the victim of some sort of magical attack, or, and most people will believe this to be the more probable explanation, was suffering from an acute attack of schizophrenia and believed herself subjected to such an attack.

Although King ends with the more likely explanation, the addition of the black cloak of Hiereus is unusual. Some allege it was an Alpha et Omega cloak, while others claim it was a Golden Dawn one, even though they are fundamentally the same. However, the two Hectors found Norah naked, and a plain cloak a few meters away.

Hiereus is Greek for 'priest' and the person who wears the cloak of Hiereus is one of three chief officers in the Golden Dawn temple. The person is stationed in the western part of the hall, the place of the fading light, opposite the Hierophant. The Hiereus is a militant, martial force within the temple and oversees the lesser officers in the execution of their duties.

During her time with the Golden Dawn, Norah was an outer guardian and would not have been a chief officer within the group. Secondly, she would not have had access to the cloak of Hiereus and would have respected the ways of the group. Upon finding the body, the two Hectors would have likely noticed if the cloak was an occult one and reported it as such.

The name of Norah is listed in the Hammersmith co-masonic lodge membership roll list for the years she was there. Norah was her motto name for the group, the same as Mac, though she wrote under Mac Tyler, not Norah. She only went by the name Norah when performing actions with the group and was only known to have gone by Norah as a nickname.

Molly Whittington-Egan, in her 1998 book "Scottish Murder Stories," states that the name of Norah Fornario is clearly listed with the names of other members of the Alpha and Omega Lodge, as established by Moina Mathers in 1919. That lodge was disbanded in 1939 on the outbreak of war.

Molly preferred the name Netta as it had a more exotic feel to it, rather than Marie or Norah. It's probably one of the reasons why Netta connects more to readers and writers, due to the name being quite different from her given names, lending it an air of mystery and exoticism that only such a name could create.

It's not uncommon for many people to be given different names by others. Nicknames are, after all, the names for which we tend to be remembered, out of affection from those around us. Perhaps it's fair that Netta is a more widely known and accepted name for her rather than her given names.

It is, of course, how many people come across her story in the first place. Although I hesitate to keep calling her Netta, preferring Norah, I appreciate that whether it is Netta or Norah, her story is still the same.

Further sensationalism comes in the form of Alisdair Marshall's familiarly titled "Scottish Murder Stories" in 1983. Alisdair describes Norah's arrival and stay on the island in a fairly similar fashion to others, but it's the death scene where the story goes sky high.

The barking of a collie drew two crofters to the death scene. She was naked apart from a long black cloak decorated with occult insignia and a blackened silver chain around her neck. He face frozen in a rictus of terror. Her toes and the balls of her feet were torn and lacerated, though the skin of the heels was intact. She had obviously been running full tilt to escape something.

Clenched, claw-like in one hand was a long steel knife. The searchers had to forcibly prise her fingers apart to retrieve it. With it, she had gouged the rough outline of a cross in the peaty turf. On this her body lay, as if in one last desperate supplication for divine mercy or protection. The call of the island had led Norah Farnario [sic] closer to Hell than Heaven.

Alasdair Marshall, Scottish Murder Stories, 1983.

To claim that Norah had obviously been running full tilt to escape something suggests that she was being chased or hunted, despite the lack of evidence or witness accounts to support such claims, aside from the embellishment of the man in the black cloak.

However, the question remains: why was Norah barefoot? It could suggest that she was experiencing a bad mental health episode, or that she felt more connected to the earth that way. Nevertheless, it is still peculiar that she left the house without shoes during the harsh weather that Iona invariably experiences in the autumn and winter months.

Interestingly, Marshall's book offers no sources or bibliography, leaving us unsure of where this assumption about Norah running from something comes from beyond pure speculation.

In 2012, a book called Ghosts & Gallows: True Stories of Crime & the Paranormal by Paul Adams, jumped all in on the occult aspect, as many books and articles in the 2000s did and continue to do.

"Norah's death was an unusual and seemingly inexplicable event that took place which has strange connections with Crowley himself, with Samuel MacGregor Mathers, with the shadowy world of Victorian occultism and, seemingly, the disturbing paranormal phenomenon of psychic attack and murder. It would be unwise to dismiss the possibility of psychic attack from beyond the grave out of hand."

Paul Adams, Ghost & Gallows.

From then on, the so-called revelations relating to Norah's death are embellished even further. It is at this point where we venture deeper into the remaining questions regarding her death and the mystery surrounding it.

The Lingering Mysteries

In 2013, a short eBook titled "The Norah Fornario Experience" by Dedemia Harding, published exclusively on Kobo, suggests that Norah was murdered by the islanders due to her extravagant ways and her connections to the occult.

> *"Officially, Norah dies of exposure, but the islanders waited two days before raising the alarm that she was missing. As a private investigator, I am of the opinion that Norah was possibly murdered by one of the islanders and there was a subsequent cover-up."*
>
> Dedemia Harding.

However, the islanders did not wait for two days. On Monday morning, the Camerons assumed that Norah had gone for a walk, and when she didn't return that night, they raised the alarm. Due to the darkness, the main search was carried out the next day, Tuesday. Her body was found early that afternoon.

While it's possible that she walked out on Sunday night, which would have put her time from leaving the house to being found at almost two days, the Camerons reacted to her disappearance one day later. Norah was known to take long walks around the island. The suggestion that the islanders killed Norah and covered up her murder is something that other articles have touched on.

But Harding goes further and suggests that "because we only have the islanders' accounts of what happened to Norah, it is conceivable that the islanders were misleading." She claims that perhaps Norah's "religious leanings and practices were the motive" or that she was the victim of a "rejected romantic crush." Harding goes on to speculate that Norah was buried under mysterious circumstances, presumably to avoid bad publicity, but it could have also been out of fear of what she represented.

Norah's burial was not mysterious and happened because the islanders banded together to raise enough funds to bury her on the island, as her family couldn't make the trip or the arrangements to collect the body. The islanders did this out of kindness, not malice or mystery. The discreet tombstone is due to her burial in the graveyard of the kings, where having any stone in or around that area is significant.

The people of Iona, as well as the Highlands and Islands of Scotland, are caring and hard-working. They tend to feel at one with their land and ancestors and are tolerant of the millions of international visitors who descend on the region each year.

The important word here is tolerance. There was no suggestion that Norah had a romantic fling on the island, and if she did, the Camerons would have known about it, and that knowledge would have been passed down to Calum Cameron.

Now, let's address the question posed by Dedemia and others who follow the same line of thinking: Did the islanders kill Norah? My belief is absolutely not, and I'll explain why. I'm primarily a researcher and writer of true crime and have come to understand much about the psychology of crime and the people who commit it.

If the islanders had decided to kill Norah or anyone on their island, it would have been illogical and risky to leave the body on the island for someone to find. And if that was the case, it would seem foolish for the two Hectors – residents of the island – to have found her body. Unless, of course, only some of the residents were involved, and the discovery could be explained away.

If they wanted to kill Norah, there would have been a simple and logical way of disposing of the body – dumping it in the ocean, into the rough seas around the island. Norah often sat on the shoreline, so it wouldn't have been too much of a stretch to suspect she either walked in or got caught up in the waves.

At least that's the story one could tell the police, when in reality, the killer or killers could have taken a small boat and dropped her body into the ocean. Given that everyone seemed to believe she was insane anyway, it wouldn't have been too difficult for the police to conclude that she had disappeared by her own hand.

It also seems unbelievable that the islanders would kill Norah, discover her body, report mysterious happenings, bring in the police, get a coroner involved, risk being caught, and then have a funeral – burying their victim on their island to be remembered for the rest of time. In all my years as a true crime researcher, this simply would not happen.

It's a grim thought, but it would be easy to dispose of a body in some parts of Scotland. The very fact that they found her body is evidence that Norah was not killed by the islanders, and the notion is mostly considered a rude one. No one could keep a secret that big for almost 100 years, especially an entire island. As with many sections of spoken or written history, we should be wary of what is taken as truth.

An article on Planet Today claims that "clutched in her hand was a sheaf of incomprehensible letters from an unidentified stranger." This is an extraordinary claim backed up by an ordinary source, a Facebook group called "Ghosts, the paranormal, supernatural, myths and legends." For the post in question, the source used there comes from another extraordinary article on a 2009 website called Lady Garotte. In that post, the following is written:

Death on Iona

> *"Norah Fornario was a victim of something very nasty, something 'Wicker Man' like and Iona Isle, along with its inhabitants, got off scot-free."*

Lady Garotte.

In the post, the author believes that Norah was hastily buried and the matter was hushed up. As the only accounts of her death come from the residents themselves, the extraordinary claim is made that Norah was sacrificed by the locals of Iona, by way of being drugged and left outside in freezing temperatures. The article ends with the belief that something sinister occurred, and that her death was brushed under the carpet.

It's worrying that something like this is seen as evidence of something sinister, spread onto a Facebook group, taken as truth, spread further, embellished eternally, and picked up by future bloggers who believe they've stumbled across a mysterious murder.

To understand the belief that Norah was killed as a result of the ritual she had supposedly been enacting, I reached out to a man who prefers to remain unnamed due to his occult affiliations. I asked him what kind of ritual Norah may have been carrying out. His response was:

"I can find no information on any ritual related to A.O. (Alpha et Omega) where it would be necessary to carve a cross into the ground and lay down on it. Nor is there any known ritual in occultism or spiritualism where carving a Christian cross into the ground is considered a pathway to the other side."

If there is no known ritual that assumes a Christian cross cut into the ground can lead through to the other side, it seems more likely, as Calum Cameron stated, that Norah was randomly stabbing at the ground for reasons that some may deem insanity. I inquired further with many self-proclaimed occultists regarding the original Golden Dawn and Alpha et Omega but was advised by almost all not to deal with anyone else I was seeking.

There is an elitism involved with some people who proclaim to be experts on the Golden Dawn. Many claim to be the first to share certain rituals or writings when, in fact, the information has been readily available for over 100 years. A small visit to the Museum of Freemasonry, where they hold much of the Golden Dawn material, will show that.

It amazes me how many "occultists" claim to *own* the Golden Dawn, when all they are doing is repeating what has gone before under a name that, to the average reader, is cloaked in mystery and misunderstanding.

Death on Iona

The Hermetic Order of the Golden Dawn ended in the early 20th century, and its last offshoot ended around the time of the Second World War. Though there is renewed interest in the occult in the 21st century, there is no ritual related to what Norah was supposed to have been enacting in 1929.

In some circles, there is confusion over the exact date of Norah's death. If she had died two days before being found, the body would have been in a state of decomposition. During the autumn and winter months, Iona and most of Scotland experience immense cold and biting frosts. If Norah had died of exposure on Sunday night and was not found until Tuesday, it remains likely that the frost had preserved the body.

An autopsy was not carried out as there was no reason to suspect murder. Only in cases where someone's death is deliberate or uncertain will an autopsy be performed. The coroner quickly pointed out that Norah had died of exposure, and aside from cuts on her feet caused by walking barefoot over scree and rock, there was no reason to suspect any foul play.

Due to the preservation of the body and the biting cold, it was impossible to accurately determine the time of death. If we accept the Camerons statement that Norah disappeared sometime on Sunday night or Monday morning, then we can assume that Norah died at some point on Monday and was discovered on Tuesday.

Questions about the man in the cloak arise. Who saw him, and when did they see him? If Norah was found dead with a black cloak nearby, is it not conceivable that someone had seen her walking around the island?

If there were no boats, how could someone else have gotten to shore without being seen in the small community that ultimately looks out to the seas? Where did they dock, and how did they contact Norah? Why were they there?

The identity of the person who saw the man in the cloak has never been uncovered, and the only evidence of it is in the news reports of the time. They do not mention where the information came from. It is possible that someone could have docked a small rowing boat on Iona without being seen, but they would have had to have come from Mull.

This would mean that someone there would have remembered or seen someone taking a boat from there. It also stands to reason that the boat would have been stolen from Mull, rather than the mystery person bringing a boat with them.

The theory of someone traveling to Iona to kill Norah seems implausible given the distances involved and the difficulty of getting to the island unseen. Although some still believe that Norah was killed by a man in a cloak who arrived on the island in the middle of the night and remained mostly unseen by the locals, it's unclear what motive this person would have had.

Was Norah privy to occult elements that she was not supposed to see? Did she hold secrets that could harm someone else, and were they worth killing for? As we have already seen, those involved in the occult are no more dangerous than those involved in mainstream religion. One could argue that those involved in mainstream religion are considerably more violent and vocal towards the occult community.

Death on Iona

The Corridors of Time

Many questions will always remain in the case of Norah Fornario but this author believes she was an emotionally damaged woman, who escaped a childhood of grief, to find solace in the occult, and it was those beliefs that exacerbated her mental collapse. Environment can influence mental states, and isolation would be an obvious example of this.

You can certainly worsen your mental state by telling yourself that psychic attacks are real and can happen at any time. In his memoirs, Aleister Crowley claimed to have been a victim of a psychic attack, and also said he had done battle with someone on the astral plane. As with all memoirs, we are led to believe that what is written is the truth.

Despite the circumstantial evidence that Norah succumbed to mental instability, there is always the slim possibility that Norah was killed by psychic attack. Who am I question to the fallacies and the inevitably of something far greater than the human condition?

In the end, the truth behind the mysterious death of Norah Fornario ultimately depends on your personal beliefs, dear reader. While I have shared my opinion, yours may differ based on the information presented in this book and beyond. And that's perfectly fine, for it would be a dull world if we all shared the same views.

Throughout thousands of years, countless books have been written on the quest for God, and this book is no different. At the heart of Norah's story lies the search for answers, redemption, and the elusive beyond of the thin place.

However, there is a more disturbing aspect to this story: how so much can be lost to the corridors of time and the annals of history. So quickly can the details of one's life be lost to the ashes of fire, the idiocy of others, accidental record-destruction, or even purposeful. As years go by, documents and records disappear, and we can only hope to create new testimonies for our future. Alas, we cannot turn back time to recover that which is lost forever, even if we wish we could.

12-year-old Calum Cameron witnessed Norah writing and typing throughout the night, voluminously. Though we know now that what she was writing has been lost to the same history as her life, there is a frustration and a depression at the heart of her story that reaches to us from the past.

Had Norah not suffered an early death then she might have been as prolific a writer as Dion Fortune or even Madame Blavatsky, and been remembered as a legend of spiritualism, rather than a footnote of an Ionian mystery, that at its heart, was not much of a mystery at all. The greatest mystery is those words she wrote in the hours and days before her demise.

Her story serves as a cautionary tale about the dangers of delving too deeply into the occult and of the consequences that can come from isolation and mental instability. However, it is also a story that speaks to the human need for answers and understanding, and the quest to uncover the mysteries of the universe.

While the details of Norah's life and death may never be fully revealed, we can take comfort in the fact that her story has not been forgotten. In fact, it continues to captivate and intrigue people to this day, as evidenced by the many theories and discussions surrounding her death.

Perhaps Norah's greatest legacy is the reminder that every life, no matter how seemingly insignificant, has the potential for great impact and contribution to the world. We can never know what insights or revelations Norah may have uncovered in her writings, but we can honour her memory by cherishing and preserving our own stories and experiences.

In a world where so much is lost to the passage of time, Norah Fornario's story serves as a reminder to cherish and preserve our own stories, and to never stop seeking the answers that can help us make sense of our place in the universe.

Where we end with no ultimate revelation about Norah's demise, we are left to wonder what great revelations she had uncovered in her writings. Though her writings and indeed most of her life are lost to history, we could use her story as a warning for our own – that story we live right now, hoping to make sense of the world around us.

A story that we will hope won't be lost to the corridors of time, like Norah's.

> *"One watches the descent of the curtain convinced that in spite of the apparent tragedy, and notwithstanding struggle, illusion and mistakes, the end is peace and fulfilment for all."*
>
> Norah Fornario.

The Legacy of Norah

When the first edition of this book was released, it served as both a test of interest in the story and a way to identify any information I may have missed. To my surprise, I received numerous emails from people from all walks of life, who had either written about Norah Fornario or Iona in relation to spirituality. It is quite fitting to include some of these pieces here, as they show how a story with minimal information from a century ago can capture imaginations across the world.

I believe that these poems and pieces of prose add a valuable perspective to the story of Norah Fornario, and I am grateful to the authors who have given me permission to reproduce their works here. While they retain all copyright to their works, I believe that sharing their words will help to create a more complete picture of the legacy that Norah has left behind.

It is my hope that these contributions will inspire others to continue exploring the mystery of Norah Fornario and the spiritual significance of Iona. As we continue to uncover new information and perspectives, we may come closer to understanding the truth behind her life and death, and the significance of her story in our own lives.

A Secret Veiled in Shadows Deep

By Marina Sky

In Iona's mystic air doth dwell, A tale that whispers ancient spell, Of Norah Fornario's enigmatic fate, Upon this isle, a mystery great.

The Scottish isle, shrouded in lore, Where monks of yore did once explore, A land of spirits, where they'd roam, In search of secrets, making home.

A lass, enchanting and so fair, Norah ventured forth, a soul aware, Of magic's touch, she sought to find, The sacred truths of humankind.

Her cloak of deep and velveteen, With silver cross, a sight serene, Upon the moor, she cast her will, To summon forces, strong and still.

A waning crescent graced the sky, As whispered winds did gently sigh, The stones of old bore witness too, To Norah's quest in twilight's hue.

Enraptured by the mystic dance, She delved within a trance-like trance, Inscribed upon the earth her plea, For wisdom vast, and secrets free.

The dawn arose with colours spread, To find the maiden cold and dead, No mortal touch, nor hand of man, Could solve the riddle of her plan.

What happened there, upon that night? Did spirits beckon, or take flight? Did unseen forces cast their snare, In Iona's grasp, so fraught with care?

The mystery of Norah Fornario, In Iona's heart, remains untold, A secret veiled in shadows deep, As silent whispers softly weep.

Seeker of Truth

From Heather Macintyre

A century ago, a story unfolded on a windswept island in Scotland, its echoes reverberating through time, whispering secrets that have inexplicably entwined themselves with my own existence. This mysterious tale of a life extinguished in the remote, rugged landscape has haunted my thoughts and stirred my soul, leaving me pondering the greater questions of life, meaning, and death.

Inexplicably drawn to this enigma, I feel an overwhelming connection to the lost history, as if the very essence of the event had seeped into my being. The island's secrets, shrouded in the mists of time, have touched me deeply, and I find myself compelled to remember and honour this unknown soul who departed from this world a century ago.

The weight of this connection has granted me a newfound appreciation for the pursuit of life, the preciousness of every breath, and the fleeting nature of our existence. It has awakened in me a yearning to delve into the depths of my own purpose, to seek out the hidden meanings that lie beneath the surface of the everyday.

It is through this journey of reflection that I have come to understand the importance of remembering, of preserving the stories that have been washed away by the sands of time. In keeping alive the memory of this mysterious death on a distant Scottish island, I am able to honour the delicate tapestry of life and to recognise the interconnectedness of all things.

And so, with every thought, every word, and every action, I weave this century-old mystery into the fabric of my own existence, allowing it to guide me as I navigate the ever-shifting landscape of life. For it is in acknowledging the significance of the past that I can truly appreciate the present and embrace the endless possibilities of the future.

A Young Enchantress

By Sage Stoneheart

In Iona's realm of tales untold, Where history whispers, secrets bold, A mystery shrouded in enigmatic mist, Norah Fornario's fate does twist.

This land of peace and sacred air, Where angels dance on churches fair, A hallowed isle, where spirits dwell, In shadows cast by ancient spell.

Norah's heart, with magic filled, Sought occult wisdom to be willed, A fairy's touch, her soul to bind, To secrets lost and truths unkind.

In Iona's grasp, a tale unfolds, Where history's voice and mystery moulds, A young enchantress, pure and bright, Stepped forth into the mystic night.

With angel's grace, she found her place, Beside the church, her spirits brace, Inscribed her plea, in soil and stone, For ancient knowledge, all her own.

By fairy's glimmer, she did dance, A sylvan scene, in moonlit trance, In peace, she reached for secrets veiled, Her spirit soared, as body failed.

The dawn awoke, with colours cast, Upon the sight of dreams now past, Norah lay still, her life withdrawn, A puzzle cloaked in shades of dawn.

What force unseen did gently trace, Her final steps in Iona's grace? Did occult powers, or angels fair, Take hold of her, in their eternal care?

A mystery lingers, whispers soft, In Iona's air, where legends waft, Norah Fornario's tale unknown, Forever etched in history's stone.

A Prayer to Angels

By Shane Friend

In misty shrouds of ocean's grace, There lies an isle with tales to trace. A hundred years have passed us by, Since whispers 'cross the sea did fly.

A tale of angels bathed in light, And a spiritual dance of endless night. There, heaven's secrets danced and swirled, Unravelling truth in a hidden world.

An island veiled in mystery's cloak, Entwined with hope and magic's yoke. The sky above, a twilight hue, A canvas painted by the island's rue.

Upon the shore, a story churned, Of tragic fate and lessons learned. A death that shook religion's core, Leaving ghosts to wander, evermore.

The pain, it lingered, whispers spoke, Of souls unbound, their fetters broke. A prayer to angels in the sky, To heal the heart that ached to die.

The ocean's waves caressed the shore, A sombre hymn forevermore. A sacred space, the island's face, Enshrined in time, a hallowed place.

In twilight's glow, the spirits yearn, For answers lost, for truth's return. The island's secrets yet untold, A mystic tale, forever bold.

Expanse of Time

By David Fraser

In the vast expanse of time, a century past, a tale of mystery unfurled on a remote island in Scotland. Its ethereal whispers tugged at my soul, drawing me closer to a story that has forever altered my perception of life, death, and the spiritual essence of the world. An inexplicable bond has formed, weaving its way through the tapestry of my being, leaving me forever connected to this enigmatic event.

The island of Iona, with its ancient history and spiritual significance, has stirred within me a deep sense of reverence and wonder. Like the ebb and flow of the tides, it has washed over me, awakening my spirit and igniting my desire to delve into the hidden truths of our world. The power of this connection has awakened in me an urgency to share this inspiration, to kindle the flames of curiosity and exploration in the hearts of others.

It is through the act of remembering and honouring this mystery that I hope to inspire a new generation of seekers, to set forth on their own journeys of discovery and understanding. The whispers of Iona call to us, urging us to delve deeper, to reach beyond the veil and to uncover the spiritual secrets that lie hidden beneath its rugged landscape.

By embracing the unknown and cherishing the power of the past, we can forge a brighter future, one where the mysteries of our world are explored and celebrated with reverence and awe. As I carry this story with me, I am compelled to share its essence with others, to honour the memory of a life lost a century ago, and to inspire the continuous pursuit of knowledge, spirituality, and self-discovery.

Let us never forget the spiritual legacy of Iona, a beacon of hope and inspiration, an eternal reminder of the interconnectedness of all things. In honouring the mysteries of the past, we can illuminate the path forward, empowering each of us to continue the journey toward enlightenment and understanding.

The Immortal Hour

The following are some of Norah Fornario's written works and additional information regarding her death. The bibliography at the end of the book provides further reading and sources cited in this book, along with copyright information and image sources.

The following essay-style pamphlet is available to read at the British Library. The piece is out of copyright and reprinted here to expand on the story of Norah and to provide further insight into the subject of this book.

In her review of the play, Norah references verbatim various scenes and dialogue which intrigue and inspire her to write about it. The full text of The Immortal Hour play and subsequent musical adaption is available to read on archive.org and other public domain sites where the text is displayed for free and also out of copyright. I highly recommend giving it a read to understand why Norah was so infatuated with it.

The title of the essay is '*The Immortal Hour, An interpretation of the play by Fiona Macleod.*' Written by Norah under the pseudonym and Alpha et Omega motto of Mac Tyler. It was first and only published by

London publisher Frederick Newman in 1923 and was only ever published in English.

Identifying features of the piece in the British Library are system number, 003698506, general Reference Collection 11795.aaa.40, and UIN: BLL01003698506.

The Immortal Hour, An interpretation of the play by Fiona Macleod.

Mac Tyler (Norah), January 1923.

During the course of some three and twenty performances of "The Immortal Hour," the writer of this booklet has gained much amusement from the comments of the audience, yet, if various remarks overheard on such occasions have enlivened the interval between the two acts with flashes of humour, (mostly unconscious on the part of the speakers), they also provided matter for considerable reflection.

Visitors to the Regent Theatre may be roughly classified as follows; students of mysticism and folk-lore who are able to understand the great truths concealed behind this gossamer curtain of faery; (a small clan, but they come frequently and every time discover some new aspect of illuminating significance), a large number of people who think the play beautiful but sad; and many for whom the whole drama is so elusive and incomprehensible that they irritably demand of each other "what on earth the fellow can be getting at," and are frankly bored: and there is a fourth class who, while keenly appreciating the artistic beauty of the performance, also sense the existence of a deeper meaning, but are hopelessly baffled by their inability to interpret the intricate symbolism employed.

It was for such seekers that this interpretation was written, and in the hope that these tentative suggestions, based on a study of comparative religion, folklore, mysticism and symbolism will provide them with the necessary clues.

While this Celtic allegory may be interpreted to represent the return of Spring to the world from the enforced thraldom of Winter, it will be apparent to all students of esoteric cults that we have here a drama similar to those employed in the ancient mysteries, and that the reactions and interaction of Dalua, Etain, Eochaid, Midir and the two peasants, symbolise the psychological and spiritual effects of initiation.

Practically all the religious systems of the ancient world, and most of the modern ones also, include two strongly differentiated types of teaching, the one exoteric, the other esoteric.

The exoteric or public side of any faith dealt with the moral precepts and ordinary religious ceremonies generally in use; the great truths underlying all religion were therein allegorised for the benefit of those who were not sufficiently evolved to grasp the fundamental philosophical concepts in their abstract form, and therefore had to be taught in terms of concrete things which are known to all.

The esoteric side dealt with the abstract philosophical concepts veiled by the exoteric symbolism. These ideas were never publicly proclaimed, but they were taught in secret all down the ages to such advanced individuals as were capable of understanding them, and who having reached a certain standard of moral, intellectual and spiritual development, were permitted to take part in the mysteries where they were instructed in the spiritual science of raising the lower self or personality to the level of the higher self or Individuality.

The allegories employed in the various exoteric systems seem to contradict each other but the esoteric interpretations are the same in every case, notwithstanding the apparent diversity of the different symbolism.

The Celtic mysteries are denoted by two mythological traditions; one is the Feast of Age, instituted by Manannan Mac Lir; the other is the Shadowy Fount of Beauty wherein the Salmon of Knowledge swims among berries fallen from the rowan, quicken tree or mountain ash, the Tree of Life in Celtic mythology, corresponding to Yggdrasil, the World Ash of the Scandinavians.

The opening speeches of the first scene of "The Immortal Hour" appertain to the world of thought; the stage is almost in darkness, vague shadows appear and disappear, denoting half-formulated concrete ideas strange and alien to Dalua, (who represents the abstract mentation of man), as that abstract mentation is itself alien to the emotions of normal humanity. The abstract mentation holds converse with half-caught intuitions which inform it that though it has travelled from one darkness to another, yet it has come…

> "no further than a rood,
> A little rood of ground in a circle
> woven."

All this first scene is tremendously significant, a clue to much that follows afterwards, and that would be otherwise be incomprehensible. The working of the principal of polarity is clearly shown in Dalua's assertion that he is…

> ". . . not first or last of the Immortal clan. For whom the long ways of the world are brief. And the short ways heavy with unimagined time."

Implying that the conditions of the physical world are reversed in the metaphysical.

Dalua, (who represents the abstract mentation of man), is recognised by the light of the wandering star above him, and the intuitions hail him, half mockingly, half fearfully,

> "….Sad Shadows of pale hopes, Forgotten dreams, madness of men's minds; Outcast among the Gods, and called the Fool, Yet dreaded even by those immortal eyes."

The Gods symbolise the highest type of emotional forces, but even these shrink from the cold impersonal detachment of the abstract mind, whose touch also wrecks the concrete mind if the latter has not been rendered sufficiently plastic by training to endure the shock of such an impact.

The chorus of intuitions now gives place to a chorus of demons symbolising the dark atavism of the subconscious forces which endeavour to acclaim the abstract mentation as part of their own evil, because the reaction of the lower principles to the mistranslated stimulus of the super-conscious frequently produces disastrous results on the material and lower emotional planes. This is why Dalua is said to bring madness and death, which generally result from misapplication of metaphysical forces.

In a marvellously orchestrated chorus of mocking laughter the demons gibe at the dreaded power who has unwittingly strayed among them. Dalua silences them with an angry gesture, bidding them laugh not,

> "For Lu and Oengus laugh not, nor the gods. Safe set above the perishable stars."

The music here explains much that is left otherwise unexpressed. In the well-night perfect beauty of the Dalua motive we have all the sadness of mortal struggle and spiritual triumph marvellously interwoven, as in one flash of supreme vision the mind visualises its own high origin and lofty destiny, and unflinchingly carries out the plans of the forces whose tool it knows itself to be. It accepts the hatred and fear of the lower principles, which are unconscious of the law with which it co-operates, and, in realisation of the sublime ultimate purpose, it has already attained in essence, even though suffering in its own application of the law to itself and others.

Dalus is a composite figure, including many of the characteristics of Lucifer, Saturn and Pan. As Lucifer he tempts Etain, even as the serpent tempted Eve, and with a similar object; as Saturn he initiates Eochaid, weighing him in the balance and warning him that those led by dreams shall be misled, for those who seek initiation guided only by emotion and not by reason, cannot pass the necessary tests. Like Pan, who brought madness and death on those who confronted him unexpectedly, at the close of the play the Fairy Fool bestows the boon of death on the heart-broken king who demands from him the restoration of his dreams. The shadow of Dalua's hand, as applied to Etain and Eochaid to bring forgetfulness, corresponds to the draught of Lethe offered to souls about to descend into incarnation. It polarises their respective attitudes; Etain is made to forget her fairy kindred and high estate; Eochaid, who symbolises the desire principle, is made to imagine himself greater than he really is, a king of dreams and shadows, instead of their plaything, and a fit mate for the immortal Star of the Shee. The Shee are the Celtic gods, the spiritual emotions of man, which appear cold and cruelly callous to the warm passions of humanity.

Etain's appearance on the stage is marked by a slight increase of light, and as she represents the soul, we may surmise that this section of the play deals with the forces of the lower emotional or desire plane; the actual change from the mental plane to the desire takes place previous to this point and is denoted by the departure of the intuitions and the entrance of the demon chorus.

Etain is half fascinated, half terrified by Dalua, who suddenly during their conversation realises why their meeting in that strange place has been ordained, and tells her of the King of Men, who has wooed the Immortal Hour, and

> ". . . sought and found and called upon the Shee. To lead his love to one more beautiful than any mortal main."

but concludes sternly that there is only

> "One way to that gate: it is not Love Aflame with all desire: but Love at peace.2

He then makes a significant gesture which is repeated at Eochaid's death. This gives us a very important clue to the cause of the tragedy. Eochaid's desire for initiation is prompted by a selfish longing to grasp and hold for himself something beyond the ordinary quality of joy, not by a desire for service, and because the motive of his quest is purely selfish, the hidden god speaking from the fountain warns him to return, but the warning is unheeded as Dalua's mocking laughter lures the king onward to his doom.

The second scene shows Etain sheltering from a storm in the hut of two peasants who represent animal instincts, and who are terrified both of her and of Eochaid, who seeks shelter from them also. The lower instincts are as much afraid of the desire principle, when that is seeking its higher self, as they are of the Soul, knowing full well that such an attempt towards unification, if successful, will inevitably be followed by an attempt at their own extinction. In this case it is not successful, as when they intreat Eochaid to do them no ill, he gives perfunctory assurances of his harmlessness towards them, while the rising tide of the great love duet surging in the orchestra denotes that he is hardly conscious of what he is saying, or of anything in all the world but the beauty of Etain.

She is equally swayed by emotion and moves towards him like one entranced, though when he kisses her hand, she breaks away, half conscious that she is transgressing. But the spell is too much for her; she yields to his passion and the love music reaches an ecstatic climax as they both sing

> "The years, the bitter years of all the world. Are now no more."

when the mockery of Dalua is heard from the orchestra, and Eochaid demands, half in anger, half in fear,

> "Who laughed? What means that laughter?"

Etain wearily seats herself at the other side of the stage, the king kneels by her side, and the two peasants slumber by the glowing fire, when suddenly a sound of far-away music is heard, and Etain rouses herself to listen to the song of the Shee. Eochaid hears nothing and is both puzzled and troubled as she turns from him, and rises from her seat, with outstretched arms, straining towards the distant voices. She has remembered something of her true nature and passionately regrets her self-determined exile.

The scene of the second act is laid in Eochaid's dun and shows us the rejoicing at the first anniversary of his wedding. After a chorus of bards and soldiers, Etain enters with her women, pale and sorrowful. During the first act, she wears the green gown of the fairy folk but now she is robed in gold and red; Eochaid who enters shortly afterwards is also robed in the red that symbolises passion, though in the first act he wears blue, the colour of aspiration.

Etain complains of weariness and announces her intention to retire, but Eochaid entreats her not to leave him, confessing that in spite of all the rejoicing he is "sore wrought by dreams and premonitions," expressed by a sinister little chromatic passage in the orchestra. He has heard again the laughter of Dalua and senses the approach of trouble, but notwithstanding his request, Etain passes out with her women, and he dismisses the rest of the court with the exception of an old bard and a page. The last two Druids on the point of departure are startled by the sudden appearance of a stranger in green, who stands in the doorway and hails the king, apologising for his late appearance and requesting a boon. Eochaid is somewhat disconcerted, but replies with dignity that

> ". . . no stranger claims a boon in vain
> . . . if that boon be. Such as I may
> grant without loss of fame. Honour or
> common weal,"

and enquires the name of the mysterious visitor. This the stranger refuses to give but proclaims his royal lineage in a passage of exquisite beauty:

Death on Iona

> "I am a King's first son. My kingdom
> lies beyond your lordly realms O King,
> and yet upon our mist white shores
> The Three Great Waves of Eire rise in
> foam. But I am under sacred bonds
> To tell no man, not even the king, My
> name and lineage. King, I wish you
> well, Lordship and lands and all your
> heart's desire."

Eochaid turns to him impulsively, then recollecting the presence of the two Druids, he dismisses them, before confessing his longing

> "To know there is no twilight hour
> Upon my day of joy."

The stranger reminds him that great poets have sung how

> "Great love survives the night and
> climbs the stars, And lives the
> Immortal Hour along the brow,
> Of that Infinitude called Youth whom
> men Name Onegus Sunrise."

Death on Iona

But Eochaid is also a poet and desires a more definite reassurance. The stranger, who is Midir, a prince of the Fairy people, husband of Etain, and symbolises the Spirit, now leaves the entrance and comes forward, flinging wide his cloak, as if announcing himself the messenger of the gods. He sings of the Immortal Hour from a Cosmic standpoint, as exemplified by Aed and Dana, suggesting the immortality of love and its Cosmic significance, but Eochaid's reaction to this clarion challenge is in terms of personality, a passionate prayer that he and he alone may keep Etain for ever, and so he misses his great opportunity.

Midir turns significantly away. Eochaid murmurs bitterly, "Dreams, dreams," and then enquires what boon is desired by his visitor. He is still more troubled when Midir asks to touch the white hand of the queen, and to sing her a song, but the king has given his word, so he sends the page to summon her, and while they await her appearance, the old bard gives definite form in the following words to the vague uneasiness pervading the whole of this scene.

> "I have seen all things pass and all things go Under the shadow of the drifting leaf; Green leaf, red leaf, brown leaf; Grey leaf blown to and fro, Blown to and fro.
>
> I have seen happy dreams rise up and pass Silent and swift as shadows on the grass Grey shadows of old dreams, Grey beauty of old dreams, Grey shadows on the grass."

The old bard slowly hobbles away, and Etain enters, clad in the green robes of the first act. She starts when Eochaid speaks to her, and complains that she could not sleep, for her dreams came close and whispered in her ears. Eochaid informs her why he has summoned her, and Midir moves from behind a pillar into her line of vision. She looks at him in bewilderment, and when he kisses her hand she starts again, as though half remembering, then recovering herself, she prays him to sing his song, and he obeys in the words and melody used by the fairy people at the close of the first act. As the notes die away she stammers confusedly,

> "I have heard, I have dreamed that song."

In the next lyric Midir declares his identity; she rushes impulsively towards him, and then draws back, confused, as she remembers her desertion of him and her own unworthiness, but still he woos her with outstretched arms, and at length she comes to him, saying,

> "I am a small green leaf in a great wood, And you are the wind o' the south"

It is significant that after kissing Etain's hand, Midir carefully refrains from touching her again, even after her surrender, implying that though the spirit may descend to woo the soul and reclaim her, it is on alien ground in the lower planes, and their true relation cannot be resumed until the soul returns to the higher level.

Eochaid here endeavours to come between them but is repulsed by a gesture from Midir, who slowly moves backwards to the entrance, drawing Etain after him. She moves as though in a trance, and to Eochaid's passionate appeals she only replies gently,

> "I cannot hear your words so far away, I go from dark to light"

and so passes out of his life, to the sound of the fairy chorus in the distance. This is the part most generally misunderstood, as the majority of people sympathise with Eochaid and feel that Etain has treated him badly.

The real clue to the situation lies in the fact that Eochaid and Midir are polarity aspects of the same principle; and therefore a unity. When Eochaid was offered his heart's desire, he could have gained the right to follow Etain to her immortal home, had he been content to sacrifice himself for her welfare, but because his love is selfish, he loses her objectively, and, though erroneously, feels that he has lost her irrevocably. If the lower nature is content to follow where the higher principles lead, it can be regenerated without suffering much of the pain entailed by its endeavour to drag down the soul; but a refusal to be regenerated necessitates its sacrifice that the soul may be liberated. Yet the lower nature and the higher are one in essence, though manifesting in opposite directions; and the death of

Death on Iona

Eochaid symbolises the metaphysical attainment of his heart's desire, since in the supreme surrender Love is at peace, as Dalua's gesture signifies, and this is the essential condition announced in the first act for all who would stand beside

> "The rainbow gate of her whom none may find, The Beauty of all Beauty."

The essence of Eochaid, all of him that is pure and great, (being almost the highest possible expression of the personality, truly a King of men,) is incorporated with the polarity aspect, Midir, and thus in the metaphysical world Midir-Eochaid hold Etain forever, and the cycle is complete. In the original play, Eochaid's entreaty to Dalua,

> "My dreams, my dreams, give me my dreams."

is answered by the significant words,

> "There is no dream save this, the dream of death."

implying that death itself is only a dream and that the ultimate reality for Eochaid, as for Midir and Etain, lies in the other world, where all life is one Life.

Death on Iona

This is not obvious to the majority of people, and it is unfortunate that this pregnant sentence was omitted; but the wonderful music of the closing bars, based on a re-statement of the Dalua theme, explains it with extraordinary clarity for those who can understand, and one watches the descent of the curtain convinced that in spite of the apparent tragedy, and notwithstanding struggle, illusion and mistakes, the end is peace and fulfilment for all.

The Use of Imagination

As with the Immortal Hour review, this fascinating piece is reprinted here to expand on the story of Norah and to provide insight into the subject of the book. This piece is an article published in the July 1928 edition of The Occult Review.

It appears in Volume 48, edition number one, and is written by Norah, again under the pseudonym and Alpha et Omega motto of Mac Tyler. The full text of this edition of Occult Review is available to read on archive.org and other public domain sites where the text is displayed for free and out of copyright.

The Use of Imagination in Art, Science and Business.

By Mac Tyler. The Occult Review v48 n1 Jul 1928.

"WHERE there is no Vision, the people perish," and where there is no imagination, there can be no Vision comprehensible to the personal self, for it is the principal function of this much misunderstood and often mistakenly abused function to interpret the abstract truths cognised by the inner spiritual Being, expressing them in terms which can be understood by the personal and outer mind.

Imagination is thus the mediator between the inner and outer selves of man; between the seen and the unseen; between those inner realities which can be spiritually apprehended, but never objectively proven, and those outer faculties which now, even as of old, seek ever for a tangible and objective sign.

Imagination is not in itself Vision, but it may be regarded as the sensitive plate by means of which Vision is made manifest; and its activities, when functioning rightly, may be described in the words of the Earth Sprit in Goethe's Faust:

> "It is thus at the roaring Loom of Time I ply, and weave for God the garment thou seest Him by."

Imagination is the vehicle of dream rather than the source thereof, being definitely a faculty of the personality; whereas for the source of dream and vision we must penetrate far beyond the persona or "mask," to the inmost mysteries of Being itself.

Imagination and Intuition are often confused by those who have not experienced the latter in its true form. This is hardly surprising, as the difference between them is most subtle, and almost impossible to describe in objective terms. Perhaps one can come near to defining them by saying that when Imagination alone is functioning, there is always a

Death on Iona

sense of becoming, whereas Intuition lifts us to realms of pure Being, unconditioned by time.

Imagination is therefore that focussing point where the powers of personality are synthesised and uplifted to contact the realities of the Divine and (relatively) formless worlds, and to clothes those realities with the interpretative qualities of form. Consequently it is at once the greatest asset and greatest danger, both to the individual and to the race.

it is the seed of genius; it is also the seed of insanity; and unless it is ensouled by inner truth and controlled by well-balanced reason, it may become a psychological cancer of stupendous dimensions, gradually absorbing all other faculties into itself, until some acute form of paranoia or dementia praecox ensues.

In the World of Art the uses of Imagination are so manifest as to need little emphasis or elaboration, but in the World of Business it is often despised, and its eminently practical value ignored.

It can never be sufficiently emphasised that the only satisfactory basis of business enterprise is an adequate appreciation of human values. This depends upon what Algernon Blackwood calls the faculty of "inside sight," feeling with people to the point of understanding their needs and cravings from the inside, even as they themselves understand them; and for this process Imagination is absolutely essential.

Blackwood's Prisoner in Fairyland is a perfect expression of spiritual truth intuitionally apprehended and embodied in the most delicate imaginative form.

Only this image-building faculty of the mind can relate and interpret to the personality that which the sensitive inner

Being registers of another's pain or need, and thus enable us to put ourselves mentally or consciously in the other person's place, to view his circumstances from his own standpoint, and to share his pain and limitation by the identification of our consciousness with his.

Such a mental process is preliminary to all true healing, either social or individual, and only by a wide and generous application of this principle can we hope to heal the terrible wounds which are poisoning social and business life-to-day.

If Capital and Labour would but strive to feel with each other, instead of striving continuously to outdo each other, many of our sorest social problems would automatically find solution, for if we truly felt the need and suffering of others as though it were out own, we should not rest, we could not rest, until that suffering had been alleviated, that need supplied.

it is because business people as a class are sadly neglectful in applying imaginative faculty (while many are actually deficient in that respect) that they are unable to translate in terms comprehensible to the personal self those realities which their inner Beings apprehend; and so, for lack of a bridge between the higher and lower selves, or between the inner and the outer, they endure existences of terrible and unnecessary psychological limitation, producing often unintentional and sometimes almost incredible brutality in human relationships, whether of the business or social world.

Many well-meaning people would be horrified beyond measure could they see and understand the cruelties of which, owing to deficiency of imaginative faculty and sympathetic insight, they are sometimes guilty. The great majority of people do not deliberately desire to give pain, and the suffering they inflict is an unconscious by-product of the self-preservation instinct, often arising from fear, which, as Galsworthy truly said, "is the black godmother of all damnable things."

On the other hand, there are cases in which, although the imaginative faculty may be well developed, it is applied in a purely negative way. In curative psychological work one often comes across such instances. In many such cases the patient's imagination is used only negatively, to enable its possessor to evade unpleasant responsibilities; or to plan for personal advancement, wholly regardless of other people's claims and their possible detriment; or sometimes even to create for its possessor some convenient ailment which shall exempt the patient from unpleasant duties, procuring him sympathetic indulgence and unremitting attention from the other members of the family circle.

Such negative and destructive forms of imaginative activity have brought into much disrepute an invaluable faculty which, rightly used, should be essentially and creatively altruistic in function, widening our sympathies, breaking down the artificial barriers of caste and clan and creed, and enabling us to meet all men and women on equal terms of frank comradeship and brotherliness.

In the world of Science, as in the world of Art, this imaginative faculty is given a far more honoured place than in the world of business; for the scientist knows that it is the pioneering faculty by the help of which all the most brilliant scientific attainments have been achieved.

The scientist checks and weighs its promptings with the utmost care, but her rarely neglects to take it into consideration as the businessman so often does, and her rarely permits it to rule him entirely as the artist so often does.

The artist's imaginative faculty is frequently in need of training and discipline, for unless it is balanced by clear reason, it is apt to distort the spiritual truths it strives to express, instead of embodying them in beautiful and helpful form. But a force misdirected is of greater evolutionary value than a force crippled, distorted, crushed almost out of existence. The misdirection is only a matter for mental education; but the healing of a withered and starved imagination is a process requiring infinitely deeper knowledge and more gradual, more far-reaching modes of service, operating not from the mental but the spiritual plane.

Where we cannot achieve counsels of perfection in our educational system, it would be infinitely wiser to permit some measure of over-development to a child's imagination, rather than to check or thwart it. Little permanent harm will result if the imaginative faculty if carefully fed on beauty of truth, nature, art, and brotherhood, even though its functions may seem for a time to be somewhat over-emphasised. Beauty may be defined as truth expressed graciously, therefore right training in the appreciation of beauty will automatically produce an innate sense of balance. True balance must always be the result of inner poise rather than of outer criticism and correction. The expression of outer criticism is often a tacit admission of our own failure to render inner sustenance to the one we criticise. All true growth and healing is from within outwards, therefore those who would minister to another's psychological need must learn to do wo from the innermost sphere where all life is realised as one in essence, though manifesting outwardly in diversity of myriad forms.

Comparatively few of us are able to realise this truth continuously as an abstract fact but aided by Imagination on the personal plane and by Intuition on the spiritual plane, and working in terms of the Law of Correspondences, we may realise it by means of analogies, and so attain in Art, Science and Business the only sound basis of practical universal brotherhood.

The true evolutionary purpose of Imagination is to enable the personality to quarry from the dull uninspiring grind of everyday life, material which shall be transformed by the alchemic action of spiritual potencies into a Universal Temple, dedicated to the glory of that sublime Indwelling Divinity, which, though sometimes latent and wholly hidden, is nevertheless immanent in every unit of Humanity.

Death on Iona

Selected Bibliography

Abergavenny Chronicle. (1909) *A GRANDFATHER'S WILL, 1909-04-16*. Abergavenny Chronicle - Welsh Newspapers. From https://newspapers.library.wales/view/4119823/4119825/19

Adams, Paul. (2012) *Ghosts & Gallows: True Stories of Crime & the Paranormal*. The History Press. ISBN: 9780752463391

Ancestry.com. *London, England, Electoral Registers, 1832-1965* [database on-line]. Provo, UT, USA: Ancestry.com Operations, Inc., 2010.

Bell, Burton. C. (1995) *Quote from Demanufacture, album by Fear Factory*. Roadrunner Records. RR 8956-2.

Blamires, Steve. (2013) *The Little Book of Great Enchantment*. Skylight Press. ISBN: 9781908011831.

Boston Record, The. (10th March 1950) *Francis Cardinal Spellman and 300 American Roman Catholic Holy Year Pilgrims arrive in Nice*. The Boston Record.

Colquhoun, Ithell. (1975) *Sword of Wisdom: MacGregor Mathers and The Golden Dawn*. Neville Spearman Ltd. ISBN: 9780399115349.

Cook, Mary, (2018) Thin Places. English Honors Theses. https://creativematter.skidmore.edu/eng_stu_schol/10

DiCamillo. (2021) *Cockley Cley Hall*. (2021). Retrieved 11th November 2021, from https://www.thedicamillo.com/house/cockley-cley-hall/

Evans-Wentz, W. Y. (1990) [1966] *The Fairy-Faith in Celtic Countries*. New York: Citadel. ISBN 0-8065-1160-5.

Fanger, Claire. (2006) *Dion Fortune. Wouter Hanegraaff Dictionary of Gnosis and Western Esotericism*. Leiden: Brill. ISBN: 9789004152311.

Fraser, David (2023) Expanse of Time.

Friend, Shane (2023) A Prayer to Angels.

Goelet, Ogden. (2015) (1500 BC) *The Egyptian Book of the Dead: The Book of Going Forth by Day : The Complete Papyrus of Ani*. Chronicle Books. ISBN: 9781452144382.

Golden Dawn Bradford. (2018) *Marie (Norah) Fornario, Jimi Hendrix and the Horus Temple of the Golden Dawn*. Golden Dawn Bradford Blog.

Halliday, Ron. (1997) *McX: Scotland's X-files*. B&W Pub. ISBN: 9781873631775.

Harding, Dedemia. (2013) *The Norah Fornario Experience*. Emily Street, United Kingdom.

Hendrix, Jimi. (1967) *The Wind Cries Mary from Are You Experienced*. Copyright Experience Hendrix LLC.

Jarron, Matthew. (2015) *Independent & Individualist: Art in Dundee 1867-1924*. Dundee: University of Dundee Museum Services/Abertay Historical Society. ISBN: 9780900019562.

Kemplay, John. (2009) *The Paintings of John Duncan: A Scottish Symbolist*. Pomegranate Artbooks. ISBN 9780764951596.

King, Francis. (1971) *The Rites of Modern Occult Magic*. New York, Macmillan. LCCN: 76158933. Republished from *Ritual Magic* in 1970. Republished as *Modern Ritual Magic: The rise of Western Occultism* in 1989.

Kisner, Jordan. (2020) *Thin Places: Essays from in Between*. Picador USA. ISBN: 9781250785909.

Knight, Gareth. (2006) *Presentation regarding Dion Fortune and early occultism*, given at Canonbury Masonic Research Centre, London, in October 2006.

Lee, Christopher. (2011) *'You'll not only lost your mind, you'll lose your soul.'* Quote from talk at University College Dublin

MacArthur, E. Mairi. (2001) *Iona*. Colin Baxter Island Guides. ISBN: 9781841070797

MacArthur, E. Mairi. (2007) *Columba's Island. Iona from Past to Present.* 2nd edn, Edinburgh University Press. ISBN: 9780748632619

Macintyre, Heather (2023) Seeker of Truth.

Macleod, Fiona. (William Sharp). (1899) *The Immortal Hour: A Drama in Two Acts.* (reprinted 1907) Thomas B. Mosher, Pennsylvania.

Marshall, Alisdair. (1983) *Alisdair Marshall's Scottish Murder Stories.* Lang Syne Publishers Ltd. ISBN: 9780946264476.

Mayo Clinic. (2021) *Pituitary Tumours - Symptoms and Causes.* Mayclinic.org. Retrieved 7th October 2021.

McNeill, Florence Marian. (1990) *An Iona Anthology.* New Iona Press. ISBN: 9780951628300. Reprinted from 1947 edition. Eneas MacKay. ISBN: 0951628305

Melville, Elizabeth. (2020) *The Strange Death of Norah Fornario.* Medium.com

Milwaukee Sentinel. (9th March 1930) *Weird Death of Scientist's Daughter Linked With Cursed Statue.* Milwaukee Sentinel, Wisconsin, United States

Original data: *Electoral Registers.* London, England: London Metropolitan Archives.

Paracelsus. Waite, Arthur Edward. (1910) (2009) *The Hermetic and Alchemical Writings of Paracelsus*. Martino Fine Books. ISBN: 9781578988341

Paradise, Viola I. (May 1918) *Death*. A Magazine of Verse. Edited by Harriet Monroe. Chicago. Vol. XII, No. II.

Paradise, Viola I. (May 1918) *Death*. Poetry: A Magazine of Verse. Chicago.

Richardson, Alan. (1987) *Priestess: The Life and Magic of Dion Fortune*. Aquarian Press. ISBN: 9780850304619.

Richardson, Alan. (2007) Priestess: *The Life and Magic of Dion Fortune*. Loughborough: Thoth Publications. ISBN: 9781870450119.

Sky, Marina (2023) A Secret Veiled in Shadows Deep.

Stoneheart, Sage (2023) A Young Enchantress

Tyler, Mac. (1923) *The Immortal Hour, An interpretation of the play by Fiona Macleod*. Frederick Newman. British Library 003698506/UIN: BLL01003698506.

Tyler, Mac. (1928) *The Use of Imagination in Art, Science and Business*. The Occult Review v48 n1 Jul 1928.

Weiner, Eric. (2012) *Thin Places, Where We Are Jolted Out of Old Ways of Seeing the World*. The New York Times. http://www.nytimes.com/2012/03/11/travel/thin-places-where-we-are-jolted-out-of-old-ways-of-seeing-the-world.html

Whittington-Egan, Molly. (1998) *Scottish Murder Stories*. Neil Wilson Publishing. ISBN: 9781897784808.

Wilson, Richard. (1989) *Scotland's Unsolved Mysteries of the Twentieth Century*. Robert Hale Ltd. ISBN: 978-0709038283.

Death on Iona

Photo of Moina Mathers in the public domain.

Photo of the pupils at Ladies College published with permission from the Des Ruelles family. The same photo is available out of copyright but should be credited to as the Ladies College, 1911.

Both of John Duncan's paintings, 1911's The Riders of the Sidhe, and 1913's St. Bride are reprinted here as both are in the public domain within the UK and U.S.

Iona Abbey and Nunnery by Caroline Hall.

The chapel near the Iona Abbey and the high cross through the arched front of Iona Abbey by Mick Haupt.

Iona from the sea by Lynda B.

Fancy a trip down true crime alley?

As a thank you for adding this book to your collection, we would like to offer you a FREE eBook for simply signing up to our mailing list. Along with a free book, you'll get weekly updates from the world of true crime brought to you by truecrimelists.com and early book release notifications so you can be the first to get them at an introductory price, exclusively for subscribers!

Visit TRUECRIMELISTS.COM and click on FREE BOOK from the menu.

Death on Iona is also available as a paperback.

Out now in bookstores worldwide or from
www.twelvetreescamden.co.uk

Death on Iona

Visit the author's website at www.writetheplanet.co.uk

For information about special discounts available
for bulk purchases, sales promotions, book signings,
trade shows, and distribution, contact
hello@twelvetreescamden.co.uk

Twelvetrees Camden Ltd
71-75 Shelton Street, Covent Garden
London, WC2H 9JQ

www.twelvetreescamden.co.uk

www.ingramcontent.com/pod-product-compliance
Lightning Source LLC
Chambersburg PA
CBHW060532100426
42743CB00009B/1502